Teacher's Edition

Lesson and Unit Assessment

Blackline Masters with Answer Key

Grade K

mheducation.com/prek12

Send all inquiries to:
McGraw Hill
8787 Orion Place
Columbus, OH 43240

ISBN: 978-1-26-459163-4
MHID: 1-26-459163-1

Printed in the United States of America.

4 5 6 7 8 9 LMN 27 26 25 24 23

Mc
Graw
Hill

mheducation.com/prek-12

Send all inquiries to:
McGraw Hill
8787 Orion Place
Columbus, OH 43240

ISBN: 978-1-26-559763-4
MHID: 1-26-559763-4

Printed in the United States of America.

4 5 6 7 8 9 LHN 27 26 25 24 23

C

Table of Contents

SRA Open Court Reading Assessment

SRA Open Court Reading focuses on helping students develop the abilities that are critical to reading with understanding. The assessments are designed to inform instruction while giving students an opportunity to practice and apply what they have learned.

The assessments that are featured in *SRA Open Court Reading* represent reasonable expectations for students at various grades. They reflect both the Common Core State Standards and the learning standards that have been adopted by various states. Research suggests that these skills are closely related to how well students learn to read a variety of texts with understanding.

SRA Open Court Reading has a four-step assessment cycle. It starts with a **Diagnostic Assessment** used for screening at the beginning of the year. Tools to monitor progress and differentiate instruction are built into each lesson. At the end of each lesson is a **Lesson Assessment**, and a **Unit Assessment** concludes each unit. A **Benchmark Assessment** is available to monitor student progress periodically over the course of the school year.

Diagnostic Assessment

A Diagnostic Assessment is included to help you identify student strengths, weaknesses, and areas of concern in the following six technical skill areas:

- Phonemic Awareness
- Phonics and Decoding
- Oral Reading Fluency
- Spelling
- Vocabulary
- Reading Comprehension

The Diagnostic Assessment can be used as an initial screener with individual students or groups of students who you observe might be lacking the prerequisite skills for the grade level. The information from the Diagnostic Assessment can then be used to inform instruction in those specific areas.

Students entering the classroom after the start of the year should be administered the Diagnostic Assessment to ascertain what grade-level material they know, in which skill areas they might need support, and whether they need immediate intervention. For example, students at this level who struggle recognizing letters and sounds are much clearer candidates for some form of intervention than students who have difficulty with unknown vocabulary words.

As students complete the progress monitoring assessments, administer the Diagnostic Assessment to students whose performance places them at risk for reading failure: students whose **Lesson and Unit Assessment** scores are below 70 percent, who have difficulty naming capital (uppercase) and small (lowercase) letters, and who struggle to differentiate between letters, words, and numbers.

Students' results on the Diagnostic Assessment will assist you in identifying a student's literacy needs and making key instructional placement decisions. Students who score below the expected level on any of the technical skill areas will need to remedy this through additional scaffolding and support provided in the **Intervention Teacher's Guide** and **Intervention Support BLMs**.

You can use the Student Assessment Record to keep track of student performance in the Diagnostic Assessment. See page T186.

Lesson and Unit Assessments

Lesson Assessments cover the content of specific lessons, and **Unit Assessments** comprise all the content that was covered in the lessons within that unit. In most cases, content is tested at least twice within a unit, adding to the reliability of the assessment process.

The primary purpose of the Lesson Assessments is to allow the teacher to monitor student progress on a regular basis. This process makes it less likely that a student will fall behind because it gives teachers the opportunity to differentiate or repeat instruction as needed.

The Unit Assessments are summative in the sense that they represent a collection of related skills and are administered at the conclusion of a number of lessons. The goal of the unit assessment is to evaluate student proficiency of previously taught skills. The results serve as a summative assessment by providing a status of current achievement in relation to student progress through the curriculum. The results of the assessments can be used to inform subsequent instruction, aid in making leveling and grouping decisions, and point toward areas in need of reteaching or remediation.

Although the assessments are tied closely to the instructional path featured in *SRA Open Court Reading*, they may also be used independently because they reflect critical reading behaviors. For example, some assessments might be used to identify students who need the kind of supplemental instruction provided within *SRA Open Court Reading*. In kindergarten, the letter reading assessments lend themselves to this purpose, as do the fluency assessments in grades 1 through 3.

Assessment Item Types

Kindergarten assessments feature the following two item types—one requires the student to respond orally, and the other requires the student to underline the correct answer. Both are within the capabilities of the majority of kindergarten-age students.

The assessments involving an oral or physical response should be administered individually. They are best suited for individual assessment because of the response mode and great variation in the writing and motor skills of kindergarten-age students. These assessments are identified in the Directions for Teacher, at the top of each assessment.

The other assessments may be administered to the whole-class or small groups of students. For these assessments, the student underlines the correct response. The exception to this rule is a student who seems to be struggling with the response mode rather than the content being assessed. These students should be assessed individually and given an opportunity to respond by underlining, pointing, or using another method that reflects the student's knowledge of the content.

Whenever an assessment is administered to the entire class or a small group, you will find it helpful to observe the students as they respond. If you notice a student struggling to respond, or the student's completed assessment score is far lower than you would expect, it may be prudent to re-administer the assessment individually. You may find it informative to administer assessments individually to students in order to observe their response competence. Or you may choose to enhance the assessment by having the child do a think-aloud and explain the reasoning underlying the responses.

Lesson Assessments should be administered as closely as possible to the completion of the lesson. This proximity will make it more likely that the assessment will measure the student's acquisition of the skill. The **Unit Assessments** should be administered close to the completion of a unit, but there is greater flexibility with the timing. The skills within a unit will have been practiced and measured several times before hand, making the Unit Assessment a reasonable measure of how well the skills have been retained.

Ideally, all students should complete all the assessments. This level of fidelity will provide the teacher with a dependable measure of students' acquisition of the most important skills. Comprehensive assessment will make it easier to identify students who are struggling, provide them with additional instruction and practice, and prevent their falling further behind.

Administering the Assessments

Review the assessments before administering them so you are familiar with the procedures. Duplicate a copy of the corresponding student assessment blackline master for each student. Directions for administering the assessments are on each page. In some cases, such as the word reading assessment, the word prompts will appear on the page.

As was mentioned earlier, some of the assessments will be administered orally from the assessment book. If a copy of a student assessment blackline master is needed for the assessment, instruction is provided in the Directions for Teacher, at the top of each assessment. In addition, you will need a blank piece of paper and a pencil for marking answers.

Choose a comfortable place to administer the assessments. There should be relatively few distractions, and you should be able to sit beside or across from the student at a table or large desk. A quiet corner of a classroom will work well.

Follow the directions for administering the assessment. As the student responds, record on the blank piece of paper the results for each item as a + or − to indicate correct or incorrect. If you are assessing more than one student at a time, be sure to write the student's name beside the responses. This will ensure that the correct scores will be recorded for each student. At the conclusion of the assessment, score and record the results.

The assessment of high-frequency words is a keystone indicator because it represents the application of phonics skills to word reading. In addition to recording the number of words correct, you will indicate if the student seemed to recognize the words automatically. This rating will reflect the student's transition from attempting to decode a word based on phonetic principles to recognizing the word automatically.

Some students will make this transition relatively quickly, while others will take longer. Even if a student reads all the words correctly but with hesitation, you may find it helpful to have the student repeat the assessment until you are confident that the words were recognized automatically.

Organizing Assessment Results

The results of assessment are most useful when they are organized in a convenient and understandable way. The Class Assessment Record begins on page T168 and the Student Assessment Record is on page T186.

Make a copy of the Student Assessment Record for each student. Enter the results of each **Lesson and Unit Assessment** after they have been completed. On a regular basis, review a student's progress. This will provide an overview of the literacy status of a given student at any time in the school year.

Next, record the results on the Class Assessment Record. The chief purpose of this record is to help you identify students who have not yet demonstrated proficiency with specific skill clusters. These students can be grouped for additional instruction and practice in the skills as needed.

Additional Resources

Progress monitoring and instructional suggestions are provided on the following pages. However, additional information is provided online in the Resource Library. Refer to the *Assessment Handbook* and the *Intervention Teacher's Guide* for instructional suggestions to help students progress toward proficiency.

The purpose of the *Assessment Handbook* is to help you manage the use of multiple assessments, interpret the results, and use that information for instructional planning. It will provide you with basic definitions and clear guidance on how test scores can be a useful resource for addressing your students' needs.

The *Intervention Teacher's Guide* and **Intervention Support BLMs** provide 15-20 minutes of instructional materials daily to reinforce and extend the core *SRA Open Court Reading* lessons. The lessons will be used with small groups of struggling readers to pre-teach or reteach key elements of the core lesson.

Performance Expectations: Lesson and Unit Assessments

Because the skills featured in *SRA Open Court Reading* are so critical to reading success, it is important that students demonstrate proficiency. Generally speaking, 80% correct is acceptable. For constrained skills like alphabet knowledge, students should eventually reach 100% correct.

Most of the assessments in kindergarten consist of five items. For these assessments, **4 out of 5** correct is acceptable.

The Letter Recognition assessments feature eight or thirteen letters in each assessment. For these assessments, **6 out of 8** or **10 out of 13** is acceptable. The Sentence Extension assessment has six items, and an acceptable performance level is **4 out of 6**.

Print Concepts assessment performance expectations are:

• Unit 2 Assessment: **14 out of 18** correct	• Unit 6 Assessment: **11 out of 14** correct
• Unit 3 Assessment: **14 out of 18** correct	• Unit 9 Assessment: **9 out of 12** correct

The High-Frequency Word assessments are based on five or ten words. Some High-Frequency Word assessments also include an automaticity rating. The acceptable level of performance is as follows:

- Five-word assessments without automaticity rating: **4 out of 5**.
- Five-word assessments with automaticity rating: **4 out of 6**.
- Ten-word assessments: **8 out of 10**.

We encourage repeated use of these assessments until students can read all of the words accurately and automatically.

In addition, you may choose to examine a student's performance on the High-Frequency Word assessments at the word level. Here are some patterns of performance you might consider.

- Misreading regular vowels and consonants suggests that the student needs more practice in reading highly decodable words.
- A student who reads highly decodable words well but has difficulty with less decodable words probably understands the most common sound-spellings. The student probably needs practice in reading common words that have uncommon sound-spellings.
- When a student reads words correctly but slowly or with hesitation, it is likely that the student lacks confidence. Paired reading with an adult or older student who reads will help to build confidence and fluency.
- Frequent self-corrections implies that the student is not yet reading automatically. Paired reading with an adult or older student who reads will help to build automaticity.

The lesson Vocabulary assessments are based on five words. For these assessments, **4 out of 5** correct is acceptable. The unit Vocabulary assessments are based on six words. For these assessments, **5 out of 6** correct is acceptable.

- The method of assessing vocabulary at the unit level is a yes-no response to an auditory prompt in which a word is used appropriately or inappropriately. This type of assessment is challenging, involves "close listening," and is a measure of how well students can access complex verbal language.
- The approach that is used for the unit vocabulary assessments engages students in an unfamiliar task because there are no visual prompts as are used in some of the lesson assessment items. The reason for the change in format is to help students develop versatility and draw on higher-level cognitive functions. Associating words with images is an essential skill, of course, but so is listening closely and associating oral language with information stored in long-term memory.

Each lesson Comprehension assessment includes four items that address the Access Complex Text strategies and Writer's Craft skills taught that week. For these assessments, **3 out of 4** correct for the combined items is acceptable. The unit Comprehension assessments are based on ten items. For these assessments, **8 out of 10** correct is acceptable. The skills associated with these categories are listed below.

- **Access Complex Text:** Cause and Effect, Classify and Categorize, Compare and Contrast, Main Idea and Details, and Sequence
- **Writer's Craft:** Story Elements (Character, Plot, and Setting), Genre Knowledge, Language Use, and Text Features

Both of these categories include skills that will prepare students to understand and enjoy what they read. The assessment formats are varied and involve close listening. Some of the items include visual prompts, while others do not. The variety of item types will inform instruction while helping students develop the versatility and cognitive processes they need to read with understanding.

Monitoring Student Progress

It is important to keep in mind that not all students learn in the same way or at the same rate. Many factors affect student progress, especially in the early grades. They include early language exposure, socioeconomic status, and other factors. Moreover, individual students may acquire some skills at a different pace than other skills. Because of these sources of variance, we suggest several strategies.

- Evaluate progress over a reasonable time frame rather than at a single point.
- Do not hesitate to re-administer the same assessment several times when additional instruction and practice are provided. Research suggests that repeated assessment does not create a familiarity effect when feedback is not provided.
- When appropriate, allow students to move to new skills rather than limiting them to instruction and practice in only the skills with which they are struggling. For example, if students have not shown proficiency with recognition of the first cluster of alphabet letters, allow them to move on to other letters while continuing to practice the first set.

One of the most beneficial practices associated with assessment is a review with the entire class. This should be undertaken only if you are sure that the assessments will not be administered again to any of the students. Once they receive feedback and clarification, the activity has lost its value as an assessment.

The review should be considered a form of practice with feedback. Simply put, you repeat the assessment, including directions, and have students respond in a think-aloud format. When necessary, you can clarify the explanation associated with the correct answer and point out how the incorrect answers are wrong if you believe this will be helpful. The most important aspect of the review is emphasizing the correct answer using academic yet understandable language.

Speak clearly and use appropriate phrasing so that the students can understand you. If necessary, clarify words or constructs in the assessment prompts that may be unfamiliar to some students. Encourage students to contribute or ask questions. This type of interaction is extremely valuable to students because it presents them with an opportunity to process academic language in a way that is meaningful and not threatening. Moreover, it may help them approach future assessments not as situations to be feared but as opportunities to demonstrate what they know.

The primary data source provided by the assessments is the total score. This is the most dependable measure of a student's performance. If a student's performance is inconsistent or far below that of the other students in the group, you may choose to do an item analysis of the student's performance on selected assessments.

The item analysis procedure is straight forward. Choose the assessments in which you are interested and examine the student's performance at the item level. One approach is to skim the relevant assessments to see if a pattern of performance is evident. For example, does the student seem to choose correct answers to the easier items in a cluster? If so, the student might understand the underlying construct but might be unfamiliar with some of the words.

Another approach is to review a given assessment and have the student do an oral think-aloud item by item. This method is extremely informative because it gives insights into the cognitive processes that a student is using to choose an answer. Perhaps the greatest benefit is that it can confirm a student's understanding of the construct associated with the assessment.

Additional information is provided online in the Resource Library. Refer to the **Assessment Handbook** and the **Intervention Teacher's Guide** for instructional suggestions to help students progress towards proficiency.

Name _____ **Date** _____ **Score** _____

Phonemic Awareness

Directions for Teacher: Make a copy of pages 1–2 from the Student Blackline Masters section for each student. Use the student's copy to record results.

Teacher: Listen to the words that I say. If they are the same, underline the first answer. The word is *yes*. If the words are not the same, underline the second answer. It is *no*.

Teacher: The words are *run* and *run*. Draw a line under the first word if they are the same or the second word if they are different . . . *run* and *run*.

1. <u>yes</u>   no

Teacher: The words are *call* and *tall*. Draw a line under the first word if they are the same or the second word if they are different . . . *call* and *tall*.

2. yes   n<u>o</u>

Teacher: The words are *bed* and *bed*. Draw a line under the first word if they are the same or the second word if they are different . . . *bed* and *bed*.

3. <u>yes</u>   no

Teacher: The words are *made* and *paid*. Draw a line under the first word if they are the same or the second word if they are different . . . *made* and *paid*.

4. yes   n<u>o</u>

Teacher: The words are *men* and *mean*. Draw a line under the first word if they are the same or the second word if they are different . . . *men* and *mean*.

5. yes   n<u>o</u>

Name _____ **Date** _____ **Score** _____

Phonemic Awareness

Teacher: This activity is about things that rhyme. Listen to what I say. I will read a word. You will underline the picture that rhymes with the word that I say. Do you have any questions? Let's begin.

Teacher: Look at the first row of pictures. The word is *wear . . . wear*. Which of these pictures rhymes with *wear . . . wear*?

6.

Teacher: Look at the next row of pictures. The word is *hook . . . hook*. Which picture rhymes with *hook . . . hook*?

7.

Teacher: Look at the next row of pictures. The word is *tall . . . tall*. Which picture rhymes with *tall . . . tall*?

8.

Teacher: Look at the next row. The word is *house . . . house*. Which picture rhymes with *house . . . house*?

9.

Teacher: Look at the last row of pictures. The word is *head . . . head*. Which picture rhymes with *head . . . head*?

10.

Name _____ **Date** _____ **Score** _____

Phonics and Decoding

Directions for Teacher: Make a copy of pages 3–4 from the Student Blackline Masters section for each student. Use the student's copy to record results.

Teacher: Listen to what I say. I am going to make a sound that a letter makes. You listen to the sound and underline the letter that makes that sound.

Teacher: The sound is /m/ . . . /m/. What letter makes that sound? /m/

1. D <u>M</u> R

Teacher: The sound is /a/ . . . /a/. Which letter makes that sound? /a/

2. P T <u>A</u>

Teacher: The sound is /d/ . . . /d/. Which letter makes that sound? /d/

3. M <u>D</u> S

Teacher: The sound is /s/ . . . /s/. Which letter makes that sound? /s/

4. <u>S</u> A K

Teacher: The sound is /p/ . . . /p/. Which letter makes that sound? /p/

5. M <u>P</u> S

Name _____ Date _____ Score _____

Phonics and Decoding

Teacher: For each row of pictures, you decide which word does not begin with the same sound as the others. Draw a line under that picture.

Teacher: The words are *bicycle, bus, rabbit*. Which word does not begin with the same sound?

6.

Teacher: The words are *can, truck, cow*. Which word does not begin with the same sound?

7.

Teacher: The words are *mask, mop, girl*. Which word does not begin with the same sound?

8.

Teacher: The words are *apple, fireman, fan*. Which word does not begin with the same sound?

9.

Teacher: The words are *tub, cat, tent*. Which word does not begin with the same sound?

10.

Oral Reading Fluency

This assessment is to be administered individually.

In this part of the diagnostic assessment, students will be asked to name letters that are put into a random grouping. You will point to the letter, and the student will say which letter it is. Go slowly enough so the child has time to think, but give no more than five to eight seconds per letter. As each child is naming the letters, you will circle the letters that he or she knows on your score sheet (page T8).

When you have finished with the letter names, look at your score sheet. Choose up to six letters that the student knows. Underline them on your score sheet. (If they do not know any letters, stop the assessment at this point.) Then point to each of those letters, and ask for the sound that the letter makes. If the student makes the correct sound, put a check beside the letter on your score sheet.

Duplicate page T7 so the students will have the letters in front of them as you ask students to name them. This page can be reused with each student that you assess. Duplicate page T8 so you have one copy for each student you assess. As you assess each student, put his or her name and today's date in the appropriate spaces. You will mark this sheet with the student's responses.

Choose a place where you and the student can sit comfortably and where you can discreetly record the answers given. Place the copy of page T7 in front of the student, and have your copy of page T8 ready to start.

Say Look at the page in front of you. This page has all the letters of the alphabet on it.

Point to the first letter on the page. [*Point to the first letter in the first row.*]

Say Starting here, I want you to tell me what each letter is. I will point to each letter in the row. We will continue down the row, and you will tell me what each letter is. When we come to the end of a row, we will drop down to the next row on the left side [*point to the first letter in row 2*] and go on. If you get to a letter that you do not know, say "I don't know." Then we will go on. Do you have any questions? Let's begin.

The student should begin to name the letters. Remember to circle the letters they name correctly on your answer sheet. If they give the incorrect letter name for a letter, do not circle it, and do not correct the student. If the student obviously does not know the letters, discontinue the assessment after row 2.

Diagnostic Assessment
Oral Reading Fluency

When the student has finished the alphabet, look at your score sheet. Choose up to six letters, and underline them on the answer sheet.

Say I have chosen a few of the letters that you know. As I point to them, I want you to tell me the *sound* that each letter makes. If you are not sure, take your best guess. If you do not know the sound, say "I don't know." Do you have any questions? Let's begin.

Point to each of the letters that you have chosen.

Say What sound does this letter say?

Do this for however many letters you have chosen. For each letter sound produced correctly, put a checkmark beside the letter. Congratulate the student on his or her work, and send him or her back with the rest of the class.

Assessment

Oral Reading Fluency

A S D F G

H J K L P

M N B V O

C X Z Q W

E R T Y I

U

Name _____ **Date** _____ **Score** _____

Oral Reading Fluency

A   S   D   F   G

H   J   K   L   P

M   N   B   V   O

C   X   Z   Q   W

E   R   T   Y   I

U

_____ 26 Letters named correctly   _____ Sounds made correctly

     Assessment

Spelling

This assessment is administered in two parts. The first part can be done with the whole group or individually. The second part should be administered individually. During this assessment, you should cover alphabet lists in your classroom.

Duplicate enough copies of page T10 for each student. To help with your recordkeeping, you can write the students' names on the sheets before distributing them.

Say On the lines on this sheet, I want you to write all the letters of the alphabet that you know. Write as neatly as you can. When you have finished, put down your pencil. Do you have any questions? You may begin.

Walk around the room to be sure the students are doing the task. When a student stops writing, ask if he or she is finished and, if so, pick up his or her paper.

Allow five to ten minutes for the students to write.

After collecting all the papers, look at each one. Circle the letters that are acceptable, and put the total on the line at the bottom of the sheet. Then underline six letters.

For the second part of the assessment, call on individual students to come meet with you. Give them their papers. You are going have them write the letters that were correct in the opposite (capital or uppercase/small or lowercase) way they wrote them.

Say I have chosen (one to six) letters that you have written. Now I am going to have you write them in a different way. [*Point to the first letter.*] This is the (capital or uppercase/small or lowercase) [name the letter]. On the line at the bottom of the sheet, write the (capital or uppercase/small or lowercase) [name of the letter.] Write as neatly as you can. If you do not know how to write the letter that way, say "I don't know," and we will go on to the next letter. Do you have any questions? Let's begin.

For each letter, say the letter's name (example: *a*), and tell them to write the (capital or uppercase/small or lowercase) form of that letter.

When you have finished, congratulate them on their hard work, and ask them to rejoin the class.

Name _____ **Date** _____ **Score** _____

Spelling

_____ letters/52   _____ (capital/small)

Name _____ **Date** _____ **Score** _____

Vocabulary

Directions for Teacher: Make a copy of pages 11–12 from the Student Blackline Masters section for each student. Use the student's copy to record results.

Teacher: Look at the first line at the top of the page. This line is for your name. Write your name on the line.

Teacher: I am going to say three words. Then I am going to name a group. I want you to underline the word that is part of that group.

Teacher: Look at the three words for number 1. They are *leaf, blue, me*. Which word is a *color*. . . a *color*? *leaf, blue, me.*

1. leaf   <u>blue</u>   me

Teacher: Look at the words for number 2. They are *fruit, bell, block*. Which word is a *food*. . . a *food*? *fruit, bell, block.*

2. <u>fruit</u>   bell   block

Teacher: Look at the three words for number 3. They are *teacher, brown, angry*. Which word is a *living thing*. . . a *living thing*? *teacher, brown, angry.*

3. <u>teacher</u>   brown   angry

Teacher: Look at the three words for number 4. They are *purple, alphabet, you*. Which word is a *color*. . . a *color*? *purple, alphabet, you.*

4. <u>purple</u>   alphabet   you

Teacher: Look at the words for number 5. They are *vegetable, lawn, bus*. Which word is a *food*. . . a *food*? *vegetable, lawn, bus.*

5. <u>vegetable</u>   lawn   bus

Name _____ **Date** _____ **Score** _____

Vocabulary

Teacher: Look at the next page.

Teacher: Look at the three words for number 6. They are *proud, block, cousin.* Which word is a *living thing. . . a living thing? proud, block, cousin.*

6. proud   block   <u>cousin</u>

Teacher: Look at the three words for number 7. They are *green, love, I.* Which word is a *color. . . a color? green, love, I.*

7. <u>green</u>   love   I

Teacher: Look at the words for number 8. They are *dog, Monday, raspberry.* Which word is a *food. . . a food? dog, Monday, raspberry.*

8. dog   Monday   <u>raspberry</u>

Teacher: Look at the three words for number 9. They are *April, friend, beside.* Which word is a *living thing. . . a living thing? April, friend, beside.*

9. April   <u>friend</u>   beside

Teacher: Look at the three words for number 10. They are *plenty, bucket, dolphin.* Which word is a *living thing. . . a living thing? plenty, bucket, dolphin.*

10. plenty   bucket   <u>dolphin</u>

Name _____ **Date** _____ **Score** _____

Comprehension

Directions for Teacher: Make a copy of pages 13–14 from the Student Blackline Masters section for each student. Use the student's copy to record results.

Teacher: Now I am going to read you some stories. For each story, you need to decide if it could happen in real life or if it could not happen in real life. After I read each story, you will underline the first answer, *real life,* or the second answer, *not real life.* Do you have any questions? Let's begin.

Teacher: *Jeff and his brother went to the beach. They both swam, built a sand castle, and got a sunburn.* If this could happen in real life, underline the first answer. If it could not happen in real life, underline the second answer.

1. <u>real life</u>   not real life

Teacher: *Mark and Sam were walking through the forest. Suddenly a fire-breathing dragon was chasing them.* If this could happen in real life, underline the first answer. If it could not happen in real life, underline the second answer.

2. real life   <u>not real life</u>

Teacher: *Polly planted a seed in her garden. The next morning, a tree grew from the seed that reached through the clouds.* If this could happen in real life, underline the first answer. If it could not happen in real life, underline the second answer.

3. real life   <u>not real life</u>

Teacher: *Ernesto had a garden in his backyard. He grew corn, beans, and lettuce for his family.* If this could happen in real life, underline the first answer. If it could not happen in real life, underline the second answer.

4. <u>real life</u>   not real life

Teacher: *Freddie the fox saw Ellen the elephant and said to her, "Ellen, you have a very long nose."* If this could happen in real life, underline the first answer. If it could not happen in real life, underline the second answer.

5. real life   <u>not real life</u>

Name _____ **Date** _____ **Score** _____

Comprehension

Teacher: Now I am going to read you a story. Then I will ask you a question. If what I ask happened at the beginning of the story, draw a line under the first answer, "beginning." If it happened in the middle of the story, underline "middle," the second answer. If it happened at the end of the story, underline "end," the last answer. Do you have any questions? Let's begin.

Teacher: *Jacob went to Tommy's house. They played kickball. Then Jacob went home.* In which part of the story did Jacob go to Tommy's house? Beginning? Underline the first answer. Middle? Underline the second answer. End? Underline the last answer.

6. beginning   middle   end

Teacher: *The Millers went to the beach. On the way home, they stopped for pretzels. Then they drove home.* In which part of the story did the Millers drive home? Beginning? Middle? End?

7. beginning   middle   end

Teacher: *The Silvas went to the grocery store and bought food. Then they got gas for their car. Later, Mr. Silva had the car washed.* In which part of the story did the Silva's get groceries? Beginning? Middle? End?

8. beginning   middle   end

Teacher: *Joe and Brian went camping. When they arrived, they put up the tent. Then they went for a hike. Finally, they gathered wood for a fire.* In which part of the story did they take a hike? Beginning? Middle? End?

9. beginning   middle   end

Teacher: *Mr. Dailey made many repairs. First, he fixed the broken window. Then he put in a new lock for the door. At the end of the day, he raked the leaves in the yard.* When did Mr. Dailey rake the leaves? Beginning? Middle? End?

10. beginning   middle   end

Assessment

Name _____ **Date** _____ **Score** ____

Letter Recognition

Directions for Teacher: Make a copy of page 15 from the Student Blackline Masters section for each student. Use the student's copy to record results.

Teacher: This activity is about letters. I am going to show you some letters on a page. I want you to read the letters out loud. Start with the top row on the left. Read the letters left to right and then move down to the second row.

d   a   h   c

f   b   g   e

Letter Recognition total _____

Assessment   **T15**

Name _____ **Date** _____ **Score** _____

Selection Vocabulary

Directions for Teacher: Make a copy of page 16 from the Student Blackline Masters section for each student. Use the student's copy to record results.

Teacher: Listen carefully to what I say. Draw a line under the answer you think is correct.

Teacher: Which picture shows the people standing *around* the car? Draw a line under the picture that shows the people standing *around* the car.

1.

Teacher: Which picture shows the dog standing in *front* of the horse? Draw a line under the picture that shows the dog standing in *front* of the horse.

2.

Teacher: Which picture shows people who are *interested* in the fish? Draw a line under the picture that shows people who are *interested* in the fish.

3.

Teacher: Which picture shows someone who is *thoughtful*? Draw a line under the picture that shows someone who is *thoughtful*.

4.

Teacher: Which picture shows that someone hit the target *sometimes*? Draw a line under the picture that shows someone hit the target *sometimes*.

5.

  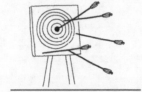 

Assessment

Name _____ Date _____ Score _____

Main Idea and Details

Directions for Teacher: Make a copy of page 17 from the Student Blackline Masters section for each student. Use the student's copy to record results.

Teacher: Look at the pictures and listen to this story. *Bees are really important. They go from one plant to another. This helps plants grow fruit that we eat.* Draw a line under the picture that shows what this story is mostly about.

1.

Teacher: Look at the pictures and listen to this story. *The boy kicked the ball. The dog chased the ball. A girl who saw them clapped her hands. The girl's father smiled.* Draw a line under the picture that shows who clapped.

2.

Story Element: Plot

Teacher: Look at the pictures and listen to this story. *Pedro found a backpack. He brought it to his teacher. The teacher put the backpack on her desk. The students came into the classroom. Rita said the backpack was hers. She said thank you to Pedro.* Draw a line under the picture that shows what happened last in this story.

1.

Teacher: Look at the pictures and listen to this story. *The woman looked at the tire. It was flat. She got the spare tire out of the car. She took the flat tire off. She put the new tire on. Then she put the flat tire in the trunk and drove away.* Draw a line under the picture that shows what happened first in this story.

2.

Name _____ **Date** _____ **Score** _____

Grammar, Usage, and Mechanics

Directions for Teacher: Make a copy of page 18 from the Student Blackline Masters section for each student. Use the student's copy to record results.

Teacher: You learned before that nouns are words that name people, places, and things. In this activity, you will find words that are people. Listen to the word I say. The word is in the box. Draw a line under "yes" if the word in the box is a person. Draw a line under "no" if it is not.

Teacher: The word in the box is *woman*. Draw a line under "yes" if the word in the box is a person. Draw a line under "no" if it is not: *woman*.

1. | woman | yes   no

Teacher: The word in the box is *store*. Draw a line under "yes" if the word in the box is a person. Draw a line under "no" if it is not: *store*.

2. | store | yes   <u>no</u>

Teacher: The word in the box is *farmer*. Draw a line under "yes" if the word in the box is a person. Draw a line under "no" if it is not: *farmer*.

3. | farmer | <u>yes</u>   no

Teacher: Now we will do something different. The names of people begin with capital letters. In this part of the activity, you will find names that should begin with capital letters.

Teacher: Look at the words: *Sit, For, Dan*. All the words begin with a capital letter, but only one is a name. Draw a line under the word that is a name and should begin with a capital letter: *Sit, For, Dan*.

4. Sit   For   <u>Dan</u>

Teacher: Look at the next group of words: *Window, Maria, Table*. All the words begin with a capital letter, but only one is a name. Draw a line under the word that is a name and should begin with a capital letter: *Window, Maria, Table*.

5. Window   <u>Maria</u>   Table

Assessment

Name _____ **Date** _____ **Score** _____

Phonemic Awareness: Word Sequence

Directions for the Teacher

This assessment is intended to be administered to students individually. Duplicate page T20 for each student you choose to assess. Write the student's name and today's date in the appropriate spaces. You will record the student's responses on this page.

Sit at a table that allows you and the student to work comfortably. You may find it easier to sit across from the student rather than beside the student.

Read the following directions:

Teacher: This activity is about first, middle, and last words. I will say three words and ask you a question about them. You will tell me the answer. Let's practice. The three words are *knife, fork, spoon*. Which is the middle word: *knife, fork, spoon*? (Allow the student to answer the question.) **The middle word was *fork*. Are you ready? Let's begin.**

Read the questions. Mark the box beside each question the student answers correctly. For ease of scoring, the correct answer is shown after the question.

After you have completed the assessment, record the number correct on the page and on the STUDENT ASSESSMENT RECORD and CLASS ASSESSMENT RECORD. If any students do not meet the recommended performance level, repeat the assessment after intervention or additional instruction.

Name _____ **Date** _____ **Score** _____

Phonemic Awareness: Word Sequence

☐ The words are *bird, fish, rabbit*. Which is the last word: *bird, fish, rabbit?*
  rabbit

☐ The words are *crayon, pencil, pen*. Which is the first word: *crayon, pencil, pen?* *crayon*

☐ The words are *bus, car, truck*. Which is the middle word: *bus, car, truck?*
  car

☐ The words are *orange, apple, pear*. Which is the first word: *orange, apple, pear?* *orange*

☐ The words are *house, school, store*. Which is the middle word: *house, school, store?* *school*

Word Sequence total _____

Assessment

Name _____   Date _____   Score _____

Letter Recognition

Directions for Teacher: Make a copy of page 21 from the Student Blackline Masters section for each student. Use the student's copy to record results.

Teacher: This activity is about letters. I am going to show you some letters on a page. I want you to read the letters out loud. Start with the top row on the left. Read the letters left to right and then move down to the second row.

n   i   p   j

m   k   o   l

Letter Recognition total _____

Name _____ Date _____ Score _____

Phonemic Awareness: Word Sequence

Directions for the Teacher

This assessment is intended to be administered to students individually. Duplicate page T23 for each student you choose to assess. Write the student's name and today's date in the appropriate spaces. You will record the student's responses on this page.

Sit at a table that allows you and the student to work comfortably. You may find it easier to sit across from the student rather than beside the student.

Read the following directions:

Teacher: This activity is about first, middle, and last words. I will say three words and ask you a question about them. You will tell me the answer. Let's practice. The three words are *knife, fork, spoon*. Which is the middle word: *knife, fork, spoon*? (Allow the student to answer the question.) **The middle word was *fork*. Are you ready? Let's begin.**

Read the questions. Mark the box beside each question the student answers correctly. For ease of scoring, the correct answer is shown after the question.

After you have completed the assessment, record the number correct on the page and on the STUDENT ASSESSMENT RECORD and CLASS ASSESSMENT RECORD. If any students do not meet the recommended performance level, repeat the assessment after intervention or additional instruction.

Name _____ **Date** _____ **Score** _____

Phonemic Awareness: Word Sequence

☐ The words are *shell, star, frog.* Which is the first word: *shell, star, frog?*
shell

☐ The words are *cat, dog, bell.* Which is the last word: *cat, dog, bell?* *bell*

☐ The words are *sun, moon, sky.* Which is the middle word: *sun, moon, sky?*
moon

☐ The words are *bat, glove, net.* Which is the last word: *bat, glove, net?* *net*

☐ The words are *cow, mouse, chicken.* Which is the first word: *cow, mouse, chicken?* *cow*

Word Sequence total _____

Name _____ Date _____ Score _____

Selection Vocabulary

Directions for Teacher: Make a copy of page 24 from the Student Blackline Masters section for each student. Use the student's copy to record results.

Teacher: Listen carefully to what I say. Draw a line under the answer you think is correct.

Teacher: Which picture shows a *counselor*? Draw a line under the picture that shows a *counselor*.

1.

Teacher: Which picture shows a *custodian*? Draw a line under the picture that shows a *custodian*.

2.

Teacher: Which picture shows where a *librarian* works? Draw a line under the picture that shows where a *librarian* works.

3.

Teacher: Which picture shows someone with a *problem*? Draw a line under the picture that shows someone with a *problem*.

4.

Teacher: Which picture shows a *secretary*? Draw a line under the picture that shows a *secretary*.

5.

Assessment

Name _____ **Date** _____ **Score** _____

Classify and Categorize

Directions for Teacher: Make a copy of page 25 from the Student Blackline Masters section for each student. Use the student's copy to record results.

Teacher: Look at the pictures for Number 1. Draw a line under the two pictures that go together because they show people working…people working.

1.

Teacher: Look at the pictures for Number 2. Draw a line under the two pictures that go together because they show things you wear…things you wear.

2.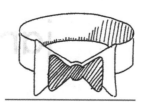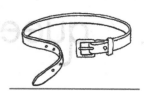

Genre Knowledge and Language Use

Teacher: You learned before that poems are a special kind of writing. Poems tell a story, and some of the words rhyme. In this activity, you will decide if this story is a poem or not. Listen to the story I read.

Teacher: *The bird flew up into the tree, and then I heard it sing to me.* If this is a poem, draw a line under "yes." If it is not, draw a line under "no." *The bird flew up into the tree, and then I heard it sing to me.*

1. <u>yes</u>   no

Teacher: Listen to the poem that I read. One word is missing from the poem. I will read the words. Draw a line under the word that fits best in the poem because it rhymes.

Teacher: The two words are *nose* and *coat*. Listen to the poem. *The best way you can smell a rose is to get real close with your…nose or coat.* Underline the word that fits best in the poem. *The best way you can smell a rose is to get real close with your…nose or coat.*

2. <u>nose</u>   coat

Assessment   **T25**

Name _____ **Date** _____ **Score** _____

Grammar, Usage, and Mechanics

Directions for Teacher: Make a copy of page 26 from the Student Blackline Masters section for each student. Use the student's copy to record results.

Teacher: You learned before that nouns are words that name people, places, and things. In this activity, you will find words that are people and things.

Teacher: Look at the words. I will say each word. I want you to draw a line under the word that is a thing: *dad, boy, house.* Draw a line under the word that is a thing: *dad, boy, house.*

1. dad   boy   house

Teacher: The words are: *queen, jar, glove.* Draw a line under the word that is a person: *queen, jar, glove.*

2. queen   jar   glove

Teacher: The words are: *mom, toy, friend.* Draw a line under the word that is a thing: *mom, toy, friend.*

3. mom   toy   friend

Teacher: The words are: *doctor, apple, baby.* Draw a line under the word that is a thing: *doctor, apple, baby.*

4. doctor   apple   baby

Teacher: The words are: *sister, button, river.* Draw a line under the word that is a person: *sister, button, river.*

5. sister   button   river

Name _____ **Date** _____ **Score** _____

Letter Recognition

Directions for Teacher: Make a copy of page 27 from the Student Blackline Masters section for each student. Use the student's copy to record results.

Teacher: This activity is about letters. I am going to show you some letters on a page. I want you to read the letters out loud. Start with the top row on the left. Read the letters left to right and then move down to the second row.

r   u   h   s

t   b   q   e

Letter Recognition total _____

Assessment

Name _____ **Date** _____ **Score** _____

Letter Recognition

Directions for Teacher: Make a copy of page 28 from the Student Blackline Masters section for each student. Use the student's copy to record results.

Teacher: This activity is about letters. I am going to show you some letters on a page. I want you to read the letters out loud. Start with the top row on the left. Read the letters left to right and then move down to the second row.

v   i   p   x

y   k   w   z

Letter Recognition total _____

Assessment

Name _____ Date _____ Date _____ Score _____

Phonemic Awareness: Rhyme Production

Directions for the Teacher

This assessment is intended to be administered to students individually. Duplicate page T30 for each student you choose to assess. Write the student's name and today's date in the appropriate spaces. You will record the student's responses on this page.

Sit beside the student at a table that allows you and the student to work comfortably. Read the directions below carefully to the student, and be sure the student understands the task. Record the student's response on the duplicated page beside the prompt word.

Teacher: I am going to say a word. I would like you to think of another word that rhymes with the word I say. The word can be real or made up.

Here's a practice word: *fan.* Can you think of a word that rhymes with *fan*?

Allow the student time to think of a rhyme. If the student cannot think of a rhyme, prompt the student with the following:

The word *can* rhymes with *fan. Can* is a real word. The word *han* also rhymes with *fan. Han* is a made-up word.

You may repeat the practice activity several more times until you are sure the student knows what to do. Some other words you may use are *bad, hit,* and *let.*

After you have completed the assessment, record the number correct on the page and on the STUDENT ASSESSMENT RECORD and CLASS ASSESSMENT RECORD. If any students do not reach the recommended performance level, repeat the assessment after intervention or additional instruction.

Name _____ Date _____ Score _____

Phonemic Awareness: Rhyme Production

Prompt	Student's Response
1. sad	_____
2. tell	_____
3. ride	_____
4. hope	_____
5. bug	_____
6. late	_____
7. meat	_____
8. fit	_____
9. top	_____
10. soon	_____

Rhyme Production total: _____

Assessment

Name _____ Date _____ Score _____

Letter Recognition

Directions for the Teacher

Pages T32–T35 should be used to assess students' knowledge of capital, or uppercase, and small, or lowercase, letter names for A through Z. This assessment is intended to be administered to students individually. Make one copy of pages T32 and T34 (uppercase letters), and T33 and T35 (lowercase letters) for each student. You will record the student's responses on each page.

Sit beside the student at a table that allows you and the student to work comfortably. Turn to page T32 or T33; provide whatever help is necessary to ensure that the student is working on the correct page. **Do not have the student mark in the book.** This will allow you to re-administer the assessment, if necessary.

Point to a letter at random, and ask the student to name that letter. Avoid pointing to the letters in alphabetical order. You should use a prompt such as "Which letter is this?" or "What is the name of this letter?" Continue the assessment as long as the student seems engaged. If possible, give the student an opportunity to respond to all the letters. Discontinue the assessment if the student is distracted, is responding randomly, or makes five errors in a row.

Use the following scoring conventions:
- Use the duplicated page to record the student's responses.
- If the student names the letter correctly on the first try, circle that letter.
- If the student names the letter incorrectly, draw an *X* over the letter.
- If the student makes an error then self-corrects, put a small question mark beside the letter. Retest the student on this letter after you have tested at least one other letter. You may use the same procedure if a student hesitates for a long time before responding or appears unsure about a letter.
- Do not allow the students to see how you have recorded their responses. Moreover, do not give them feedback about answers being correct or wrong.
- After you have tested all the letters and retested those for which the student provided an uncertain response, record the number correct, the number wrong, and the number that remain uncertain in the spaces below and on the STUDENT ASSESSMENT RECORD and CLASS ASSESSMENT RECORD. If any students do not meet the recommended performance level, repeat the assessment after intervention or additional instruction.

Assessment

Name _____ **Date** _____ **Score** _____

Letter Recognition

I D F

C G K

J A L

H B E

M

Number Correct: _____
Number Wrong: _____
Number Uncertain: _____

Name _____   Date _____   Score ___

Letter Recognition

f   d   l

k   b   g

c   i   j

h   e   a

m

Number Correct: _____
Number Wrong: _____
Number Uncertain: _____

Name _____ **Date** _____ **Score** _____

Letter Recognition

N U Q

R X T

W S O

Z V Y

P

Number Correct: _____
Number Wrong: _____
Number Uncertain: _____

Name _____ **Date** _____ **Score** _____

Letter Recognition

u   o   r

q   x   z

w   v   n

p   y   †

s

Number Correct: ____
Number Wrong: ____
Number Uncertain: ____

Assessment

Name _____ Date _____ Score _____

Selection Vocabulary

Directions for Teacher: Make a copy of page 36 from the Student Blackline Masters section for each student. Use the student's copy to record results.

Teacher: Listen carefully to what I say. Draw a line under the answer you think is correct.

Teacher: Which picture shows someone making a *speech*? Draw a line under the picture that shows someone making a *speech*.

1.

Teacher: Which picture shows a *whole* orange? Draw a line under the picture that shows a *whole* orange.

2.

Teacher: Which picture shows an animal with *hooves*? Draw a line under the picture that shows an animal with *hooves*.

3.

Teacher: Which picture shows *recess*? Draw a line under the picture that shows *recess*.

4.

Teacher: Which picture shows *sharing*? Draw a line under the picture that shows *sharing*.

5.

Assessment

Name _____ **Date** _____ **Score** _____

Compare and Contrast

Directions for Teacher: Make a copy of page 37 from the Student Blackline Masters section for each student. Use the student's copy to record results.

Teacher: The picture in the box is an apple. Draw a line under the other picture of something that is like the apple because you eat it.

1.

Teacher: The picture in the box shows a boy reading quietly. Draw a line under the picture of something that is *not* quiet.

2.

Story Elements

Teacher: Look at the pictures and listen to this story. *The bear was hungry. It saw some berries on a bush. The bear started to eat the berries. Then a bird flew by. The bear looked at the bird but did not stop eating. The berries were too good.* Draw a line under the picture of the main character in this story.

1.

Teacher: Listen to the next story. *Carla was walking her dog. She waved at her friend Dan. Dan was raking leaves. Carla and the dog went to the park. They ran around and then came home. They saw Dan again. He was still raking leaves.* Draw a line under the character who did not go to the park.

2.

Name _____ Date _____ Score _____

Grammar, Usage, and Mechanics

Directions for Teacher: Make a copy of page 38 from the Student Blackline Masters section for each student. Use the student's copy to record results.

Teacher: The word is *school*. Does this word name a place? Draw a line under *yes* or *no*.

1. 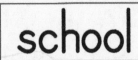 yes no

Teacher: The word is *read*. Does this word name a thing? Draw a line under *yes* or *no*.

2. 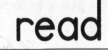 yes no

Teacher: The word is *mother*. Does this word name a person? Draw a line under *yes* or *no*.

3. 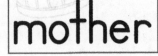 yes no

Teacher: The word is *run*. Does this word name a thing? Draw a line under *yes* or *no*.

4. yes no

Teacher: The word is *horse*. Does this word name an animal? Draw a line under *yes* or *no*.

5.  yes no

Name _____ Date _____ Score _____

Listening for Sounds

Directions for Teacher: Duplicate page T39 for each student you choose to assess. You will record the results on this page.

Gather enough materials to make four sounds. One sound will be used for practice and the other three sounds with questions 1-3. Reuse these three sounds for questions 4-5. Examples of ounds you might use are: dropping a book, paper being torn, snapping fingers, a keyboard being typed on, zipping a jacket, cutting with scissors, or bouncing a ball. Choose the sounds and record them below.

Teacher: Tell students to close their eyes to listen to the sound you will make. Make or play one sound. Then have students identify the sound, using a complete sentence such as: *I heard the sound of a _____.* Are you ready? Let's begin.

Teacher: Listen to this sound. (Make or play the sound.) What sound did you hear?

1. ☐ Sound: _____

I heard the sound of _____.

Teacher: Listen to this sound. (Make or play the sound.) What sound did you hear?

2. ☐ Sound: _____

I heard the sound of _____.

Teacher: Listen to this sound. (Make or play the sound.) What sound did you hear?

3. ☐ Sound: _____

I heard the sound of _____.

Teacher: Listen carefully to the sounds and say what they are. (Make or play two sounds.)
What was the *first* sound you heard? What was the *last* sound you heard?

4. ☐ Sound 1: _____ ☐ Sound 2: _____

First, I heard _____. Last, I heard _____.

Teacher: First, listen carefully to the sounds and say what they are. (Make or play two sounds.)
Now you are going to listen for the missing sound. (Make or play only one sound.)
Which sound is missing?

5. ☐ Sound 1: _____ ☐ Sound 2: _____

☐ Missing Sound: _____

The missing sound is _____.

Name _____ **Date** _____ **Score** _____

Listening for Words

Directions for Teacher: Duplicate page T40 for each student you choose to assess. Record results on this page.

Teacher: Listen to these words: *bird, fish, snake.* What word do you hear first: *bird, fish, snake?*

1. ☐ bird

Teacher: Listen to these words: *run, jump, swim.* What word do you hear last: *run, jump, swim?*

2. ☐ swim

Teacher: Listen to these words: *car, truck, bus.* What word do you hear in the middle: *car, truck, bus?*

3. ☐ truck

Teacher: Listen to these words: *orange, apple, pumpkin.* What word do you hear last: *orange, apple, pumpkin?*

4. ☐ pumpkin

Teacher: Listen to these words: *mother, father, sister.* What word do you hear in the middle: *mother, father, sister?*

5. ☐ father

Name _____ **Date** _____ **Score** _____

Rhyming Words

Directions for Teacher: Duplicate page T41 for each student you choose to assess. Record results on this page.

Teacher: Listen to these words: *red, bed*. Do the words rhyme: *red, bed*?

1. ☐ yes

Teacher: Listen to these words: *have, hill*. Do the words rhyme: *have, hill*?

2. ☐ no

Teacher: Listen to these words: *table, cable*. Do the words rhyme: *table, cable*?

3. ☐ yes

Teacher: Listen to these words: *side, wide*. Do the words rhyme: *side, wide*?

4. ☐ yes

Teacher: Listen to these words: *stung, stuck*. Do the words rhyme: *stung, stuck*?

5. ☐ no

Name _____ Date _____ Score _____

Vocabulary

Directions for Teacher: Make a copy of page 42 from the Student Blackline Masters section for each student. Use the student's copy to record results.

Teacher: Listen carefully to what I say. Draw a line under the answer you think is correct.

Teacher: The word is *familiar*. A stranger is a *familiar* person. Draw a line under "yes" or "no." A stranger is a *familiar* person.

1.   yes   <u>no</u>

Teacher: The word is *interested*. If you are *interested* you want to know more about something. Draw a line under "yes" or "no." If you are *interested* you want to know more about something.

2.   <u>yes</u>   no

Teacher: The word is *colorful*. A *colorful* sweater is dull and gray. Draw a line under "yes" or "no." A *colorful* sweater is dull and gray.

3.   yes   <u>no</u>

Teacher: The word is *librarian*. A *librarian* works in a library. Draw a line under "yes" or "no." A *librarian* works in a library.

4.   <u>yes</u>   no

Teacher: The word is *community*. In a *community*, people live near one another. Draw a line under "yes" or "no." In a *community*, people live near one another.

5.   <u>yes</u>   no

Teacher: The word is *hooves*. Horses have *hooves*. Draw a line under "yes" or "no." Horses have *hooves*.

6.   <u>yes</u>   no

Name _____ **Date** _____ **Score** _____

Comprehension

Directions for Teacher: Make a copy of pages 43-44 from the Student Blackline Masters section for each student. Use the student's copy to record results.

Teacher: Listen carefully to what I say. Draw a line under the answer you think is correct. Look at the pictures. Draw a line under the two pictures that go together because they show people playing sports...playing sports.

1.

Teacher: Look at the pictures. Draw a line under the two pictures that show things that are tools...things that are tools.

2.

Teacher: Now we will do something different. Look at the pictures and listen to this story. *Jamal is building a birdhouse. He is using pieces of wood and tools. When he is finished, he will put it outside near some trees.* Draw a line under the picture that shows what this story is mostly about.

3.

Teacher: Look at the pictures and listen to this story. *The mail carrier put the package on the porch. Then she went next door and put some letters in the mailbox. She put her gloves on because it was getting cold.* Draw a line under the picture that shows what was on the porch.

4.

Teacher: Look at the pictures and listen to this story. *The hikers were going up a mountain. They decided to stop and eat a snack. They found a shady spot and ate the snack. They also drank some juice.* Draw a line under the picture that shows something that is most like what the hikers did.

5.

Name _____ **Date** _____ **Score** _____

Comprehension

Teacher: Look at the pictures and listen to this story. *A cat was asleep in the chair. It heard a sound and ran to the door. Then it ran to the kitchen. Mom picked up the cat and gave it a hug. Dad shut the door.* Draw a line under the picture that shows what happened in the middle of this story.

6.

Teacher: Look at the pictures and listen to this story. *Grandfather was walking in the park with Karen. They saw Officer Miller. She waved to them. Then she walked over to some steps. She helped a woman in a wheelchair down the steps.* Draw a line under the picture that shows who Officer Miller helped.

7.

Teacher: In this activity, you will decide if this story is a poem or not. Listen to the story I read. *Looking up into the sky, the tiny mouse wished she could fly.* If this is a poem, draw a line under "yes." If it is not, draw a line under "no." *Looking up into the sky, the tiny mouse wished she could fly.*

8.　<u>yes</u>　　　no

Teacher: Listen to the poem that I read. One word is missing from the poem. I will read the words. Draw a line under the word that fits best in the poem because it rhymes. The two words are *bed* and *fox*. Listen to the poem. *A bird stood on a pile of rocks. It looked around and saw a...bed* or *fox.* Underline the word that fits best in the poem. *A bird stood on a pile of rocks. It looked around and saw a...bed* or *fox.*

9.　 bed　　　<u>fox</u>　　

Teacher: The two words are *pan* and *key*. Listen to the poem. *In the kitchen was a man who put some food into a...pan* or *key.* Underline the word that fits best in the poem. *In the kitchen was a man who put some food into a...pan* or *key.*

10.　 pan　　　key

　　　　　　　　　　　　Assessment

Name _____ **Date** _____ **Score** _____

Grammar, Usage, and Mechanics

Directions for Teacher: Make a copy of page 45 from the Student Blackline Masters section for each student. Use the student's copy to record results.

Teacher: Look at the three words: *Clock, Alice, Bottle*. All the words begin with a capital letter, but only one is a name. Draw a line under the word that is a name and should begin with a capital letter: *Clock, Alice, Bottle*.

1. Clock   <u>Alice</u>   Bottle

Teacher: Look at the words. I will say each word. I want you to draw a line under the word that is a thing: *plant, cook, zoo*. Draw a line under the word that is a thing: *plant, cook, zoo*.

2. <u>plant</u>   cook   zoo

Teacher: The words are: *stair, rug, child*. Draw a line under the word that is a person: *stair, rug, child*.

3. stair   rug   <u>child</u>

Teacher: The words are: *desert, sailor, button*. Draw a line under the word that is a place: *desert, sailor, button*.

4. <u>desert</u>   sailor   button

Teacher: The words are: *beach, deer, sink*. Draw a line under the word that is an animal: *beach, deer, sink*.

5. beach   <u>deer</u>   sink

Name _____ **Date** _____ **Score** _____

Counting Words in Sentences

Directions for Teacher: Make a copy of page 46 from the Student Blackline Masters section for each student. Use the student's copy to record results.

Teacher: This activity is about words in sentences. Listen carefully to the sentence I say. Draw a line under the number of words in the sentence. The answers are 2, 3, or 4.

Teacher: How many words are in this sentence? *Ben went home.*

1.   2   <u>3</u>   4

Teacher: How many words are in this sentence? *Hello, Ann.*

2.   <u>2</u>   3   4

Teacher: How many words are in this sentence? *Pedro can read.*

3.   2   <u>3</u>   4

Teacher: How many words are in this sentence? *This is my house.*

4.   2   3   <u>4</u>

Teacher: How many words are in this sentence? *The dog is brown.*

5.   2   3   <u>4</u>

Assessment

Name _____ Date _____ Score _____

Identifying Spoken Sentences

Directions for Teacher: Duplicate page T47 for each student you choose to assess. Record results on this page.

Teacher: Listen to this sentence: *Carlos was sitting on a horse.* What was Carlos sitting on?

1. ☐ a horse

Teacher: Listen to this sentence: *The cat saw a mouse.* What is the last word in the sentence? *The cat saw a mouse.*

2. ☐ mouse

Teacher: Listen to this sentence: *Jan came home.* How many words are in the sentence? *Jan came home.*

3. ☐ 3

Teacher: Listen to these sentences: *The car had a flat tire. The truck had a flat tire.* What word changed in the sentences?

4. ☐ car or truck

Teacher: Listen to this sentence: *A duck can fly.* Tell me what the sentence would be if you changed *fly* to *swim?*

5. ☐ A duck can swim.

Assessment

Name _____ **Date** _____ **Score** _____

Alphabet Sequence, Part 1

Page T49 should be used to assess students' knowledge of the alphabet sequence. This assessment is intended to be administered individually. Duplicate page T49 for each student you choose to assess. You will record the student's responses on this page.

Sit at a table that allows you and the student to work comfortably. You may find it easier to sit beside the student. Turn to page T49. **Do not have the student mark in the book.** This will allow you to re-administer the assessment, if necessary.

Teacher: This page has some of the letters of the alphabet. Some of the letters are missing. I would like you to say the missing letters of the alphabet in the correct order. Let's do the first row together. The two letters are *a* and *b*. What letter comes next in the alphabet? *(pause)* **The letter *c* comes next, so I will write the letter *c* in the space. Do you understand what you are supposed to do? Now, I will read the rest of the letters. Tell me the missing letters in the order they appear in the alphabet. If you think about the alphabet song, it will help you.**

After you have completed the assessment, record the number correct at the top of the page and on the STUDENT ASSESSMENT RECORD and CLASS ASSESSMENT RECORD. If any students do not meet the recommended performance level, repeat the assessment after intervention or additional instruction.

Name _____ **Date** _____ **Score** _____

Alphabet Sequence

a   b   ___

d   ___   f

___   ___   i

j   ___   ___

Assessment

Name _____ **Date** _____ **Score** _____

Selection Vocabulary

Directions for Teacher: Make a copy of page 50 from the Student Blackline Masters section for each student. Use the student's copy to record results.

Teacher: Listen carefully to what I say. Draw a line under the answer you think is correct.

Teacher: Which picture shows a ladder *against* a house? Draw a line under the picture that shows a ladder *against* a house.

1.

Teacher: Which picture shows people *arguing*? Draw a line under the picture that shows people *arguing*.

2.

Teacher: Which student *competed* in a sport? Draw a line under your answer. Which student *competed* in a sport?

3.

Teacher: Which picture shows *excitement*? Draw a line under the picture that shows *excitement*.

4.

Teacher: Which picture shows something that is *hollow*? Draw a line under the picture that shows something *hollow*.

5.

Assessment

Name _____ **Date** _____ **Score** _____

Sequence

Directions for Teacher: Make a copy of page 51 from the Student Blackline Masters section for each student. Use the student's copy to record results.

Teacher: Listen to this story and look at the pictures for Number 1. *The wolf was curled up taking a nap. It woke up and stretched. The wolf saw the rest of the pack nearby. They were howling, so it decided to howl, too.* Draw a line under the picture that shows what happened last in this story.

1.

Teacher: Move down to Number 2 and listen to this story. *Rosa opened the package of clay. She shaped the clay into a bowl. She let it dry for a few hours. Then she drew flowers on the bowl with special paint.* Draw a line under the picture that shows what happened second in this story.

2.

Genre Knowledge: Folktale

Teacher: Look at the answers for Number 1. Listen to this story. You must decide if it is a folktale. *The wise owl landed on the man's hand. The owl told the man a secret.* If this is part of a folktale, draw a line under "yes." If it is not, draw a line under "no." *The wise owl landed on the man's hand. The owl told the man a secret.*

1. yes   no

Teacher: Move down to Number 2 and listen to this story. *The scientist looked into the telescope. She saw a comet in the night sky.* If this sounds like a folktale, draw a line under "yes." If it is not, draw a line under "no." *The scientist looked into the telescope. She saw a comet in the night sky.*

2. yes   no

Name _____ **Date** _____ **Score** _____

Grammar, Usage, and Mechanics

Directions for Teacher: Make a copy of page 52 from the Student Blackline Masters section for each student. Use the student's copy to record results.

Teacher: Listen carefully to the directions in this activity. Look at the sentence for Number 1. If you were reading this sentence, which word would you start with? Draw a line under the word you would read first in this sentence.

1. Many stars are in the sky.

Teacher: Look at the sentences for Number 2. If you were reading these sentences, which one would you read second? Draw a line under the sentence you would read second.

2. The dog chased the ball.
She picked up the ball.
Then she ran with the ball.

Teacher: Move down to Number 3. We will do something different now. The three words are *run, cloud, blue.* Draw a line under the describing word...the describing word. *Run, cloud, blue.*

3. run   cloud   blue

Teacher: Move down to Number 4. The three words are *pretty, beach, swim.* Draw a line under the describing word...the describing word. *Pretty, beach, swim.*

4. pretty   beach   swim

Teacher: Move down to Number 5. The words are *music, loud, sing.* Draw a line under the describing word...the describing word. *Music, loud, sing.*

5. music   loud   sing

               Assessment

Name _____ **Date** _____ **Score** _____

Substituting Words in Rhymes

Directions for Teacher: Duplicate page T53 for each student you choose to assess. Record results on this page.

Teacher: Listen to this rhyme. *The man had a fan.* Can you think of another word that rhymes with *man* that can take the place of *fan*?

1. ☐ Answers may include can, van, or plan.

Teacher: Listen to this rhyme. *The bed is red.* Which word can take the place of *bed* in the rhyme, *shed* or *ship*?

2. ☐ shed

Teacher: Listen to this rhyme. *Take care of the chair.* Can you think of another word that rhymes with *care* that can take the place of *chair*?

3. ☐ Answers may include bear, pear, or hair.

Teacher: Listen to this rhyme. *Did you stop to shop?* Which word can take the place of *shop* in the rhyme, *mop* or *move*?

4. ☐ mop

Teacher: Listen to this rhyme. *Mom gave Doug a hug.* Which word can take the place of *hug* in the rhyme, *jug* or *jump*?

5. ☐ jug

Name _____ Date _____ Score _____

Alphabet Sequence, Part 2

Page T55 should be used to assess students' knowledge of the remainder of the alphabet sequence. This assessment is intended to be administered individually. Duplicate page T55 for each student you choose to assess. You will record the student's responses on this page.

Sit at a table that allows you and the student to work comfortably. You may find it easier to sit beside the student. Turn to page T55. **Do not have the student mark in the book.** This will allow you to re-administer the assessment, if necessary.

Teacher: This page is similar to the one you did earlier. Now we will look at the rest of the alphabet. Some of the letters are missing. I would like you to say the missing letters of the alphabet in the correct order. Let's do the first row together. The two letters are *m* and *n*. What letter comes next in the alphabet? *(pause)* **The letter *o* comes next, so I will write the letter *o* in the space. Do you understand what you are supposed to do? Now, I will read the rest of the letters. Tell me the missing letters in the order they appear in the alphabet. If you think about the alphabet song, it will help you.**

After you have completed the assessment, record the number correct at the top of the page and on the STUDENT ASSESSMENT RECORD and CLASS ASSESSMENT RECORD. If any students do not meet the recommended performance level, repeat the assessment after intervention or additional instruction.

Alphabet Sequence

m   n   ___

___   q   ___

___   ___   u

v   ___

y   ___

Name _____ **Date** _____ **Score** _____

Word Part Blending

Directions for Teacher: Duplicate page T56 for each student you choose to assess. Record results on this page.

Teacher: In this activity, I am going to say the parts of a word. Then I want you to put the parts together and tell me the word. Are you ready? *foot* (pause for two seconds) *ball*

1. ☐ football

Teacher: Put these word parts together and tell me the word. Are you ready? *some* (pause for two seconds) *times*

2. ☐ sometimes

Teacher: Put these word parts together and tell me the word. *birth* (pause for two seconds) *day*

3. ☐ birthday

Teacher: Put these word parts together and tell me the word. *after* (pause for two seconds) *noon*

4. ☐ afternoon

Teacher: Put these word parts together and tell me the word. *snow* (pause for two seconds) *flake*

5. ☐ snowflake

Assessment

Name _____ **Date** _____ **Score** _____

Selection Vocabulary

Directions for Teacher: Make a copy of page 57 from the Student Blackline Masters section for each student. Use the student's copy to record results.

Teacher: Listen carefully to what I say. Draw a line under the answer you think is correct.

Teacher: Which picture shows people who *expect* a bus? Draw a line under the picture that shows people who *expect* a bus.

1.

Teacher: Which picture shows a *fellow*? Draw a line under the picture that shows a *fellow*.

2.

Teacher: Which picture shows a *hearth*? Draw a line under the picture that shows a *hearth*.

3.

Teacher: Which picture shows a *piece* of a watermelon? Draw a line under the picture that shows a *piece* of a watermelon.

4.

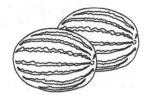 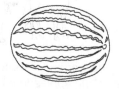 

Teacher: Which picture shows someone *helping*? Draw a line under the picture that shows someone *helping*.

5.

Cause and Effect

Directions for Teacher: Make a copy of page 58 from the Student Blackline Masters section for each student. Use the student's copy to record results.

Teacher: Look at the pictures for Number 1 and listen to this story. *Nicole wanted to read a magazine. She put her pen and glasses down and got the magazine. She sat down without looking and broke her glasses. Oh, no!* Draw a line under the picture that shows the effect of Nicole sitting down without looking.

1.

Teacher: Move down to Number 2. *Jorge saw a hole in a tree and didn't know how it got there. He saw a squirrel in the tree and a mouse beside the tree. Then a woodpecker landed in the tree. The bird pecked at the hole. Now Jorge knew what happened.* Draw a line under the thing that caused the hole in the tree.

2.

Text Features

Teacher: Look at the illustrations for Number 1 and listen to this question. *Which illustration would go best with a story about farm animals?* Draw a line under the illustration that would go best with a story about farm animals.

1.

Teacher: Look at the words for Number 2. The words are *wonder, friend, tree*. Now listen to this story. *Amina and her brother climbed a tree. They picked some apples to bring home.* Draw a line under the word that tells what a good illustration for the story would be. *Wonder, friend, tree.*

2. wonder   friend   tree

Assessment

Name _____ **Date** _____ **Score** _____

Grammar, Usage, and Mechanics

Directions for Teacher: Make a copy of page 59 from the Student Blackline Masters section for each student. Use the student's copy to record results. Read aloud the answer choices.

Teacher: Listen carefully to the questions in this activity. Think about what I say before choosing your answers.

Teacher: Look at the answers for Number 1. Draw a line under the answer that is just a letter, not a word. Draw a line under the letter.

1. the   b̲   at

Teacher: Look at the answers for Number 2. Draw a line under the answer that is a word, not just a letter. Draw a line under the word.

2. f̲o̲r̲   c   g

Teacher: Move down to Number 3. We will do something different now. The three words are *play, dog, and.* Draw a line under the action word…the action word. *Play, dog, and.*

3. p̲l̲a̲y̲   dog   and

Teacher: Move down to Number 4. Look at the words. The three words are *boat, wet, swim.* Draw a line under the action word…the action word. *Boat, wet, swim.*

4. boat   wet   s̲w̲i̲m̲

Teacher: Look at the words for Number 5. The three words are *tired, pull, down.* Draw a line under the action word…the action word. *Tired, pull, down.*

5. tired   p̲u̲l̲l̲   down

Name _____ Date _____ Score ____

Syllable Blending and Segmentation

Directions for Teacher: Duplicate page T60 for each student you choose to assess. Record results on this page.

Teacher: In this activity, I am going to say the syllables of a.word. Then I want you to put the syllables together and tell me the word. Are you ready? *prin* (pause for two seconds) *cess*

1. ☐ princess

Teacher: Put these syllables together and tell me the word. Are you ready? *draw* (pause for two seconds) *ing*

2. ☐ drawing

Teacher: Put these syllables together and tell me the word. *un* (pause for two seconds) *til*

3. ☐ until

Teacher: This activity is a little different. I am going to say a word. Then I want you to tell me the syllables that are in the word. Are you ready? The word is *picture...picture*. Say the syllables in *picture*.

4. ☐ pic ture

Teacher: The word is *turtle...turtle*. Say the syllables in *turtle*.

5. ☐ tur tle

Assessment

Name _____ **Date** _____ **Score** _____

Selection Vocabulary

Directions for Teacher: Make a copy of page 61 from the Student Blackline Masters section for each student. Use the student's copy to record results.

Teacher: Listen carefully to what I say. Draw a line under the answer you think is correct.

Teacher: Where does a *nurse* work? Draw a line under the picture that shows where a *nurse* works.

1.

Teacher: Which picture shows a *place*? Draw a line under the picture that shows a *place*.

2.

Teacher: Which picture shows a hat that is worn *properly*? Draw a line under the picture that shows a hat that is worn *properly*.

3.

Teacher: Which picture shows a *young* person? Draw a line under the picture that shows a *young* person.

4.

Teacher: Which picture shows something that is *magnificent*? Draw a line under the picture that shows something that is *magnificent*.

5.

Name _____ **Date** _____ **Score** ____

Main Idea and Details

Directions for Teacher: Make a copy of page 62 from the Student Blackline Masters section for each student. Use the student's copy to record results.

Teacher: Look at the pictures for Number 1 and listen to this story. *The family was playing a board game on the dining room table. They wore funny hats and had popcorn for a snack. It was something they did every Friday night.* Draw a line under the picture that shows what this story is mostly about.

1.

Teacher: Move down to Number 2. *People loved to visit the castle. There was a big courtyard with a fountain in the middle. It even had a tall tower and a drawbridge that you walked on to get into the castle. Visitors thought the fountain was the best part of the castle.* Draw a line under the thing that visitors liked best about the castle.

2.

Story Elements

Teacher: Listen to this story for Number 1. You must decide if it is takes place in the country. *Annie patted her favorite goat. Then she headed to the coop to collect eggs.* If it takes place in the country, draw a line under "yes." If it does not, draw a line under "no." *Annie patted her favorite goat. Then she headed to the coop to collect eggs.*

1. yes   no

Teacher: Look at the pictures for Number 2. I will ask you where this story takes place. *Antarctica is a cold and snowy place. Not many plants or animals live there. Penguins live where the ice ends and the ocean begins.* Draw a line under the picture that shows where this story takes place.

2.

Assessment

Name _____ Date _____ Score _____

Grammar, Usage, and Mechanics

Directions for Teacher: Make a copy of page 63 from the Student Blackline Masters section for each student. Use the student's copy to record results.

Teacher: In this activity, you will listen to words and decide if they rhyme. Words that rhyme end with the same sounds.

Teacher: Listen to these two words for Number 1: *sing* and *ring.* If the words rhyme, underline "yes." If not, underline "no." *Sing* and *ring.*

1. <u>yes</u>   no

Teacher: Move down to Number 2. The words are *truck* and *car.* If the words rhyme, underline "yes." If not, underline "no." *Truck* and *car.*

2. yes   <u>no</u>

Teacher: Move down to Number 3. The words are *out* and *nose.* If the words rhyme, underline "yes." If not, underline "no." *Out* and *nose.*

3. yes   <u>no</u>

Teacher: Move down to Number 4. The words are *snow* and *throw.* If the words rhyme, underline "yes." If not, underline "no." *Snow* and *throw.*

4. <u>yes</u>   no

Teacher: Look at the answers for Number 5. The words are *make* and *lake.* If the words rhyme, underline "yes." If not, underline "no." *Make* and *lake.*

5. <u>yes</u>   no

Assessment

Name _____ Date _____ Score _____

Word Part Blending

Directions for Teacher: Duplicate page T64 for each student you choose to assess. Record results on this page.

Teacher: In this activity, I am going to say the parts of a word. Then I want you to put the parts together and tell me the word. Are you ready? *side* (pause for two seconds) *walk*

1. ☐ sidewalk

Teacher: Put these word parts together and tell me the word. Are you ready? *day* (pause for two seconds) *time*

2. ☐ daytime

Teacher: Put these word parts together and tell me the word. Are you ready? *out* (pause for two seconds) *side*

3. ☐ outside

Teacher: Put these word parts together and tell me the word. Are you ready? *gold* (pause for two seconds) *fish*

4. ☐ goldfish

Teacher: Put these word parts together and tell me the word. Are you ready? *back* (pause for two seconds) *pack*

5. ☐ backpack

Name _____ **Date** _____ **Score** _____

Syllable Blending and Segmentation

Directions for Teacher: Duplicate page T65 for each student you choose to assess. Record results on this page.

Teacher: In this activity, I am going to say the syllables of a word. Then I want you to put the syllables together and tell me the word.

Are you ready? *pur* (pause for two seconds) *pose*

1. ☐ purpose

Teacher: In this activity, I am going to say the syllables of a word. Then I want you to put the syllables together and tell me the word. Are you ready? *read* (pause for two seconds) *ing*

2. ☐ reading

Teacher: This activity is a little different. I am going to say a word. Then I want you to tell me the syllables that are in the word. Are you ready? The word is *pencil...pencil.* Say the syllables in *pencil.*

3. ☐ pen cil

Teacher: The word is *table...table.* Say the syllables in *table.*

4. ☐ ta ble

Teacher: The word is *research...research.* Say the syllables in *research.*

5. ☐ re search

Name _____ **Date** _____ **Score** _____

High-Frequency Words

Directions for Teacher: Make a copy of page 66 from the Student Blackline Masters section for each student. Use the student's copy to record results.

Teacher: This activity is about words you have learned. Listen carefully to what I say. Draw a line under the word you think is correct.

Teacher: The word is *a*. *He found a ball*. Draw a line under *a*.

1. a   had   I

Teacher: The word is *he*. *He is my father*. Draw a line under *he*.

2. has   he   the

Teacher: The word is *I*. *I am happy*. Draw a line under *I*.

3. and   a   I

Teacher: The word is *you*. *When will you go home?* Draw a line under *you*.

4. you   he   has

Teacher: The word is *has*. *Alan has class now*. Draw a line under *has*.

5. and   has   he

Name _____ Date _____ Score _____

High-Frequency Words

Directions for Teacher: Make a copy of page 67 from the Student Blackline Masters section for each student. Use the student's copy to record results.

Teacher: The word is *the*. *I saw the game.* Draw a line under *the*.

6. one   how   <u>the</u>

Teacher: The word is *and*. *She and I went to school.* Draw a line under *and*.

7. <u>and</u>   not   all

Teacher: The word is *go*. *I will go there soon.* Draw a line under *go*.

8. do   <u>go</u>   of

Teacher: The word is *see*. *Can you see the players?* Draw a line under *see*.

9. <u>see</u>   are   but

Teacher: The word is *had*. *Mitch had five dollars.* Draw a line under *had*.

10. as   <u>had</u>   by

Name _____ **Date** _____ **Score** _____

Print Concepts

Directions for Teacher

This assessment is intended to be administered individually using *Pickled Peppers*. As an option, assessment may be based on observations made during regular classroom activities with any available book.

Duplicate page T68 for each student you choose to assess. You will record the student's responses on this page. Sit at a table that allows you and the student to work comfortably. Put the book on the table with the cover down. Ask the questions below and check each question the student answers correctly.

☐ Show me the front cover of this book.

☐ Show me the back cover of this book.

☐ If you were going to read this book, how would you hold it?

(For the following three items, be sure the cover of the book or the title page is showing.)

☐ Point to the title of the book.

☐ Show me the name of the person who wrote the book, the author.

☐ Now show me the name of the person who drew the pictures in the book, the illustrator.

(Turn to the table of contents page.)

☐ Can you tell me what this page is for?

(For the following questions, have the student open the book to a typical two-page spread with an illustration.)

☐ Open the book. Show me a page number.

☐ Point to a word on the page.

☐ How about a letter? Point to a letter for me.

☐ Point to an illustration on the page. An illustration is a picture.

☐ Point to a space between words. How about another space between words?

☐ Run your finger under a sentence. Show me where the sentence begins and ends.

☐ Now point to a space between two sentences. Can you show me another space between two sentences?

☐ If you were reading this page, show me the word you would read first.

☐ Now show me the words you would read next. Move your fingers to show me the direction you would read the words.

☐ After you finish reading the first line on this page, point to the line you would read next and where you would start reading.

☐ If you were reading this page, show me the word you would read last before turning to the next page.

Print Concepts total: _____

Name _____ **Date** _____ **Score** _____

Vocabulary

Directions for Teacher: Make a copy of page 69 from the Student Blackline Masters section for each student. Use the student's copy to record results.

Teacher: Listen carefully to what I say. Draw a line under the answer you think is correct.

Teacher: The word is *decided*. If you *decided*, you picked one thing rather than another. Draw a line under "yes" or "no." If you *decided*, you picked one thing rather than another.

1. <u>yes</u>   no

Teacher: Move down to Number 2. The word is *hollow*. If something is *hollow*, it is filled about halfway. Draw a line under "yes" or "no." If something is *hollow*, it is filled about halfway.

2. yes   <u>no</u>

Teacher: Look at Number 3. The word is *expect*. When you *expect* something, you think it will happen. Draw a line under "yes" or "no." When you *expect* something, you think it will happen.

3. <u>yes</u>   no

Teacher: Number 4. The word is *withered*. A wet towel is *withered*. Draw a line under "yes" or "no." A wet towel is *withered*.

4. yes   <u>no</u>

Teacher: Move down to Number 5. The word is *helping*. If you are *helping* are you being useful? Draw a line under "yes" or "no." The word is *helping*. If you are *helping* are you being useful?

5. <u>yes</u>   no

Teacher: The word is *certain*. If you think you know the answer to a question, you are *certain*. Draw a line under "yes" or "no." If you think you know the answer to a question, you are *certain*.

6. <u>yes</u>   no

Comprehension

Directions for Teacher: Make a copy of pages 70–71 from the Student Blackline Masters section for each student. Use the student's copy to record results.

Teacher: In this activity, you will answer questions about stories that I read. Listen carefully to the question and think about what I say before choosing an answer.

Teacher: Look at the pictures for Number 1 and listen to this story. *Dexter is a big, furry dog. His family also has a small dog and a cat. On cold nights, the little dog and cat snuggle against Dexter because he is so big and warm. Dexter doesn't mind at all.* Draw a line under the picture that shows what this story is mostly about.

1.

Teacher: Move down to Number 2. *Birds build different kinds of nest. A swallow lives in a nest made of mud. The mud comes from the bank of a river or lake. The swallow builds the nest against the side of a wall.* Draw a line under the kind of home that a swallow builds.

2.

Teacher: Look at the pictures for Number 3 and listen to the story. *Steve got ready for school. He put his coat on and got his backpack. He started out the door but stopped. He grabbed his hat and put it on. Then he went outside to wait for the school bus.* Draw a line under the thing that Steve grabbed just before he went outside.

3.

Teacher: Move down to Number 4. This question is a little different, so listen carefully. *Mina looked at the little mound of dirt on the ground. She wondered what made it. She thought maybe it was an ant or a beetle. Her teacher looked at it and said it was a worm. Mina was happy that there were worms in the class garden.* Draw a line under the picture that shows what caused the little mound of dirt.

4.

Teacher: Look at the pictures for Number 5. Listen to the story. *The rain fell for days. The wind blew the roof off a house. Lightning hit a tree. So much water was in the lake that the dam broke. Water rushed down the stream.* Draw a line under the effect of the all the water in the lake.

5.

Name _____ Date _____ Score _____

Comprehension, Genre Knowledge, and Story Elements

Teacher: Look at the illustrations for Number 6 and listen to this question. *Which illustration would go best with a story about exploring space?* Draw a line under the illustration that would go best with a story about exploring space.

6.

Teacher: Move down to Number 7. Listen to this story. You must decide if it is a folktale. *A microscope lets you look at things that are very small. A telescope lets you look at things that are very far away.* If this is a folktale, underline "yes." If it is not, draw a line under "no." *A microscope lets you look at things that are very small. A telescope lets you look at things that are very far away.* Is this story a folktale?

7. yes   no

Teacher: Move down to Number 8. Listen to this story and decide if it is a folktale. *The fox glared at the crow. "I will have to teach this rude bird a lesson," he said to himself.* Is the story a folktale, *yes* or *no?* *The fox glared at the crow. "I will have to teach this rude bird a lesson," he said to himself.*

8. yes   no

Teacher: Move down to Number 9. Listen to this story and think about where it takes place. *Long ago, a family lived in a log cabin. They cooked food in a fire that burned wood. They raised their own vegetables.* Draw a line under the picture that shows the setting for this story.

9.

Teacher: Move down to Number 10. I am going to read a story. You have to decide if it takes place in a school. *Enzo pushed his cart up to the counter. He waited for the cashier to tell him how much to pay.* Does this story take place in a school, *yes* or *no?* *Enzo pushed his cart up to the counter. He waited for the cashier to tell him how much to pay.*

10. yes   no

Name _____ **Date** _____ **Score** _____

Grammar, Usage, and Mechanics

Directions for Teacher: Make a copy of page 72 from the Student Blackline Masters section for each student. Use the student's copy to record results. Read aloud the answer choices.

Teacher: Look at the answers for Number 1. Draw a line under the answer that is just a letter, not a word. Draw a line under the letter.

1. say   no   <u>m</u>

Teacher: Look at the sentence for Number 2. If you were reading this sentence, which word would you start with? Draw a line under the word you would read first in this sentence.

2. <u>Some</u> ducks flew over the pond.

Teacher: Move down to Number 3. We will do something different now. The three words are *skate, cold, ice.* Draw a line under the describing word…the describing word. *Skate, cold, ice.*

3. skate   <u>cold</u>   ice

Teacher: Look at the answers for Number 4. Now you will find the action word. The three words are *climb, tree, leaf.* Draw a line under the action word…the action word. *Climb, tree, leaf.*

4. <u>climb</u>   tree   leaf

Teacher: Move down to Number 5. Listen to these two words: *soup* and *bowl.* If the words rhyme, underline "yes." If not, underline "no." *Soup and bowl.*

5. yes   <u>no</u>

Name _____ **Date** _____ **Score** _____

Blending Word Parts

Directions for Teacher: Duplicate page T73 for each student you choose to assess. Record results on this page.

Teacher: In this activity, I am going to say the parts of a word. Then I want you to put the parts together and tell me the word. Are you ready? /s/ (pause for two seconds) *at*

1. ☐ sat

Teacher: Put these word parts together and tell me the word. Are you ready? /j/ (pause for two seconds) *ump*

2. ☐ jump

Teacher: Put these word parts together and tell me the word. Are you ready? /m/ (pause for two seconds) *ake*

3. ☐ make

Teacher: Put these word parts together and tell me the word. Are you ready? /pl/ (pause for two seconds) *ay*

4. ☐ play

Teacher: Put these word parts together and tell me the word. Are you ready? /ch/ (pause for two seconds) *ip*

5. ☐ chip

Name _____ **Date** _____ **Score** _____

Phoneme Matching: Initial Sounds

Directions for Teacher: Duplicate page T74 for each student you choose to assess. Record results on this page.

Teacher: Listen to these words: *sit bit sun*. Which two words begin with the same sound? *sit bit sun*

1. ☐ sit, sun

Teacher: Listen to these words: *can red ran*. Which two words begin with the same sound? *can red ran*

2. ☐ red, ran

Teacher: Listen to these words: *dip dog log*. Which two words begin with the same sound? *dip dog log*

3. ☐ dip, dog

Teacher: Listen to these words: *fun paw far*. Which two words begin with the same sound? *fun paw far*

4. ☐ fun, far

Teacher: Listen to these words: *kite feet fire*. Which two words begin with the same sound? *kite feet fire*

5. ☐ feet, fire

Assessment

Name _____ Date _____ Score _____

Selection Vocabulary

Directions for Teacher: Make a copy of page 75 from the Student Blackline Masters section for each student. Use the student's copy to record results.

Teacher: Listen carefully to what I say. Draw a line under the answer you think is correct.

Teacher: Which picture shows *Earth*? Draw a line under the picture that shows *Earth*.

1.

Teacher: Which picture shows where you would find *information*? Draw a line under the picture that shows where you would find *information*.

2.

Teacher: Which picture shows how to *measure* something? Draw a line under the picture that shows how to *measure* something.

3.

Teacher: Which picture shows a *tool*? Draw a line under the picture that shows a *tool*.

4.

Teacher: Which picture shows *weather*? Draw a line under the picture that shows *weather*.

5.

Name _____ **Date** _____ **Score** _____

Classify and Categorize

Directions for Teacher: Make a copy of page 76 from the Student Blackline Masters section for each student. Use the student's copy to record results.

Teacher: In this activity, we will think about how things are the same and how they are different. Listen carefully to what I say.

Teacher: Look at the pictures for Number 1. Draw a line under the two pictures that go together because they show things you drink. Draw a line under the things you drink.

1.

Teacher: Look at the pictures for Number 2. Draw a line under the two pictures that go together because they are kinds of weather. Draw a line under the things that show weather.

2.

Text Features

Teacher: Look at the images and listen to this question. *Which picture would go best with a story about sailboats on the ocean?* Draw a line under the image that would go best with a story about sailboats on the ocean.

1.

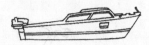   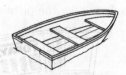   

Teacher: Listen to this sentence from a story. *Eli and Darius rode their bikes down the street.* Would a picture of a swimming pool go with this story? If it would, draw a line under "yes." If it would not, draw a line under "no." *Eli and Darius rode their bikes down the street.* Would a picture of a swimming pool go with this story? Draw a line under "yes" or "no."

2. <u>yes</u>   <u>no</u>

Name _____ Date _____ Score _____

Grammar, Usage, and Mechanics

Directions for Teacher: Make a copy of page 77 from the Student Blackline Masters section for each student. Use the student's copy to record results.

Teacher: Look at the sentence for Number 1. Count the number of spaces between the words in the sentence. Draw a line under the number that shows how many spaces there are in the sentence.

1. A bird flew by.   2   <u>3</u>   4

Teacher: Move down to Number 2. How many spaces are there in the sentence? Draw a line under the number that shows how many spaces there are in the sentence.

2. The car stopped.   <u>2</u>   3   4

Teacher: Move down to Number 3. Count the number of spaces in the sentence. Draw a line under the number that shows how many spaces there are in the sentence.

3. What time is it?   2   <u>3</u>   4

Teacher: Move down to Number 4. Count the number of spaces in the sentence. Draw a line under the number that shows how many spaces there are in the sentence.

4. I like cats and dogs.   2   3   <u>4</u>

Teacher: Move down to Number 5. Count the number of spaces in the sentence. Draw a line under the number that shows how many spaces there are in the sentence.

5. How are you today?   2   <u>3</u>   4

Assessment

Name _____ **Date** _____ **Score** _____

Phoneme Blending: Final Sounds

Directions for Teacher: Duplicate page T78 for each student you choose to assess. Record results on this page.

Teacher: Put these word parts together and tell me the word. Are you ready? *mi* (pause for two seconds) /s/

1. ☐ miss

Teacher: Put these word parts together and tell me the word. Are you ready? *gu* (pause for two seconds) /m/

2. ☐ gum

Teacher: Put these word parts together and tell me the word. Are you ready? *sa* (pause for two seconds) /d/

3. ☐ sad

Teacher: Put these word parts together and tell me the word. Are you ready? *ga* (pause for two seconds) /p/

4. ☐ gap

Teacher: Put these word parts together and tell me the word. Are you ready? *cu* (pause for two seconds) /p/

5. ☐ cup

Assessment

Name _____ **Date** _____ **Score** _____

Letter Sounds

Directions for Teacher: Make a copy of page 79 from the Student Blackline Masters section for each student. Use the student's copy to record results.

Teacher: This activity is about letter sounds. Listen carefully to what I say. Draw a line under the letter you think is correct.

Teacher: The word in the box should be *sit*. Which letter should go at the beginning of the word *sit*? Underline the letter, and make the sound.

1. 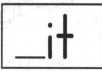   p   m   s̲

Teacher: The word in the box should be *dot*. Which letter should go at the beginning of the word *dot*? Underline the letter, and make the sound.

2. 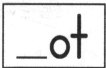   s   p   d̲

Teacher: The word in the box should be *cap*. Which letter should go at the end of the word *cap*? Underline the letter, and make the sound.

3. 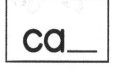   s   m

Teacher: The word in the box should be *him*. Which letter should go at the end of the word *him*? Underline the letter, and make the sound.

4.    d   m̲   s

Teacher: The word in the box should be *bed*. Which letter should go at the end of the word *bed*? Underline the letter, and make the sound.

5. 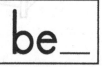   m   s   d̲

Assessment

Name _____ **Date** _____ **Score** _____

Selection Vocabulary

Directions for Teacher: Make a copy of page 80 from the Student Blackline Masters section for each student. Use the student's copy to record results.

Teacher: Listen carefully to what I say. Draw a line under the answer you think is correct.

Teacher: Which picture shows *steam*? Draw a line under the picture that shows *steam*.

1.

  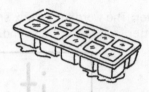

Teacher: Which picture shows an animal making a *burrow*? Draw a line under the picture that shows an animal making a *burrow*.

2.

Teacher: Which picture shows an animal that likes to *dangle*? Draw a line under the picture that shows an animal that likes to *dangle*.

3.

Teacher: Which picture shows a *tunnel*? Draw a line under the picture that shows a *tunnel*.

4.

Teacher: Which picture shows something on which you can *cruise*? Draw a line under your answer. Would you *cruise* on a chair, boat or bed?

5.

Assessment

Name _____ **Date** _____ **Score** _____

Compare and Contrast

Directions for Teacher: Make a copy of page 81 from the Student Blackline Masters section for each student. Use the student's copy to record results.

Teacher: In this activity, we will think about how things are the same or different.

Teacher: Look at the picture for Number 1. The picture in the box is a fork. Draw a line under the picture of something that is like the fork because you use it for eating.

1.

Teacher: Look at the picture for Number 2. The picture in the box is a chair. Draw a line under the picture of something that is like the chair because you can sit on it.

2.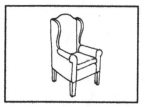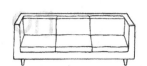

Teacher: Now we'll do a different activity. We will think about how things are the same or different.
Teacher: Listen carefully. *Is a cat more like a dolphin than a kitten?* Draw a line under "yes" or "no." *Is a cat more like a dolphin than a kitten?*

3.   no

Teacher: Listen carefully. *Is a clock more like a watch than a tree?* Draw a line under "yes" or "no." *Is a clock more like a watch than a tree?*

4.   no

Name _____ **Date** _____ **Score** _____

Grammar, Usage, and Mechanics

Directions for Teacher: Make a copy of page 82 from the Student Blackline Masters section for each student. Use the student's copy to record results.

Teacher: Look at the sentence for Number 1 as I read it out loud. *This is a pretty lake.* Should this sentence end with a period because it is declarative? Draw a line under "yes" or "no." *This is a pretty lake.*

1. This is a pretty lake

<u>yes</u>   no

Teacher: Move down to Number 2. Look at the sentence as I read it out loud. *When will the game start?* Should this sentence end with a period? Draw a line under "yes" or "no." *When will the game start?*

2. When will the game start

yes   <u>no</u>

Teacher: For Numbers 3, 4, and 5, look at each sentence. If the sentence starts with a capital letter, draw a line under "yes." If it does not start with a capital letter, draw a line under "no." Does the sentence start with a capital letter?

3. oceans have salty water.

yes   <u>no</u>

4. some parks have lakes.

yes   <u>no</u>

5. That house is very old.

<u>yes</u>   no

Assessment

Name _____ **Date** _____ **Score** _____

Letter Sounds

Directions for Teacher: Duplicate page T83 for each student you choose to assess. Record results on this page.

Teacher: Listen to this sound: /a/ What letter makes the sound /a/?

1. ☐ a

Teacher: Listen to this word: *tap*. What sound do you hear in the middle of the word?

2. ☐ /a/

Teacher: Listen to these words: *lip map top*. Which word has the /a/ sound? *lip map top*.

3. ☐ map

Teacher: Listen to these sounds and make a word from them: /b/ /a/ /t/

4. ☐ bat

Teacher: Listen to this: *h o t* spells *hot*. If you change the *o* to *a*, what new word do you have? *h o t*, change *o* to *a*.

5. ☐ hat

Name _____ Date _____ Score _____

Blending Initial Sounds

Directions for Teacher: Make a copy of page 84 from the Student Blackline Masters section for each student. Use the student's copy to record results.

Teacher: This activity is about blending sounds to make words. Listen carefully to what I say. Draw a line under the picture whose name I say.

Teacher: /d/ ish. Draw a line under the /d/ ish.

1.

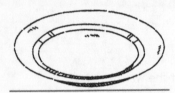  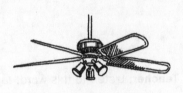

Teacher: /s/ un. Draw a line under the /s/ un.

2.

Teacher: /m/ op. Draw a line under the /m/ op.

3.

Teacher: /d/ esk. Draw a line under the /d/ esk.

4.

Teacher: /p/ en. Draw a line under the /p/ en.

5.

  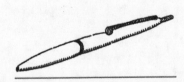

Assessment

Name _____ **Date** _____ **Score** _____

High-Frequency Words

Directions for Teacher: Make a copy of page 85 from the Student Blackline Masters section for each student. Use the student's copy to record results.

Teacher: This activity is about words you have learned. Listen carefully to what I say. Draw a line under the word you think is correct.

Teacher: The word is *we. We made lunch.* Draw a line under *we.*

1. <u>we</u>   of   am

Teacher: The word is *am. I am leaving.* Draw a line under *am.*

2. you   <u>am</u>   and

Teacher: The word is *you. Will you put the bag in the car?* Draw a line under *you.*

3. go   <u>you</u>   of

Teacher: The word is *of. The shirt is made of cotton.* Draw a line under *of.*

4. <u>of</u>   in   he

Teacher: The word is *has. She has the keys.* Draw a line under *has.*

5. had   <u>has</u>   the

Assessment

UNIT 3 • Lesson 3 (continued)

Name _____ Date _____ Score _____

Selection Vocabulary

Directions for Teacher: Make a copy of page 86 from the Student Blackline Masters section for each student. Use the student's copy to record results.

Teacher: Listen carefully to what I say. Draw a line under the answer you think is correct.

Teacher: Which picture shows someone who is *cozy*? Draw a line under the picture that shows someone who is *cozy*.

1.

Teacher: Which picture shows a *fort*? Draw a line under the picture that shows a *fort*.

2.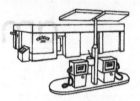

Teacher: Which picture shows a *pile*? Draw a line under the picture that shows a *pile*.

3.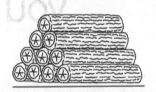

Teacher: Which picture shows something *soft*? Draw a line under the picture that shows something *soft*.

4.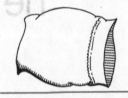

Teacher: Which picture shows a *stack* of something? Draw a line under the picture that shows a *stack* of something.

5.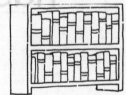

Assessment

Name _____ Date _____ Score _____

Cause and Effect

Directions for Teacher: Make a copy of page 87 from the Student Blackline Masters section for each student. Use the student's copy to record results.

Teacher: Look at the pictures and listen to this story. *The storm had lots of lightning. A bolt of lightning hit the ground and started a fire in a field. Some firefighters had to put the fire out.* Draw a line under the picture that shows what caused the fire.

1.

Teacher: Look at the pictures and listen to this story. *Bill was in a hurry. He put his coat on and ran through the kitchen. On the way, he knocked a glass over and broke it. He jumped on his bike and started to ride down the street.* Draw a line under the picture that shows what happened because Bill was in a hurry.

2.

Story Elements

Teacher: Look at the pictures and listen to this story. *A baby deer is called a fawn. It is small and has spots. As it grows older, the fawn loses its spots. When it is fully grown, it will grow antlers on its head if it is a boy deer.* Draw a line under the picture that shows what happened first in this story.

1.

Teacher: Look at the pictures and listen to this story. *The bear woke up from a long winter's sleep. It walked out of its den. The hungry bear found some plants and ate them, roots and all. Then the bear looked for a friend.* Draw a line under the picture that shows what happened in the middle of this story.

2.

Name _____ **Date** _____ **Score** _____

Grammar, Usage, and Mechanics

Directions for Teacher: Make a copy of page 88 from the Student Blackline Masters section for each student. Use the student's copy to record results.

Teacher: You learned before that declarative sentences begin with a capital letter and end with a period. In this activity, you will look for capital letters and periods.

Teacher: Look at the sentence for Number 1 while I read it out loud. *A robin is a kind of bird.* If the sentence begins with a capital letter and ends with a period, underline "yes." If not, underline "no." Does the sentence begin with a capital letter and end with a period? *Yes* or *no.*

1. a robin is a kind of bird

yes   <u>no</u>

Teacher: Look at the sentence for Number 2 while I read it out loud. *Fish can breathe under water.* If the sentence begins with a capital letter and ends with a period, underline "yes." If not, underline "no." Does the sentence begin with a capital letter and end with a period? *Yes* or *no.*

2. Fish can live under water.

<u>yes</u>   no

Teacher: Look at the sentence for Number 3 while I read it out loud. *A canyon is a kind of deep valley.* If the sentence begins with a capital letter and ends with a period, underline "yes." If not, underline "no." Does the sentence begin with a capital letter and end with a period? *Yes* or *no.*

3. A canyon is a kind of deep valley

yes   <u>no</u>

Teacher: Look at the sentence for Number 4 while I read it out loud. *A comet is something in space.* If the sentence begins with a capital letter and ends with a period, underline "yes." If not, underline "no." Does the sentence begin with a capital letter and end with a period? *Yes* or *no.*

4. a comet is something in space.

yes   <u>no</u>

Teacher: Look at the sentence for Number 5 while I read it out loud. *Your heart moves blood in your body.* If the sentence begins with a capital letter and ends with a period, underline "yes." If not, underline "no." Does the sentence begin with a capital letter and end with a period? *Yes* or *no.*

5. Your heart moves blood in your body.

<u>yes</u>   no

Assessment

Name _____ **Date** _____ **Score** _____

Letters and Sounds

Directions for Teacher: Make a copy of page 89 from the Student Blackline Masters section for each student. Use the student's copy to record results.

Teacher: This activity is about the sounds that letters make. Listen carefully to what I say. Draw a line under the answer you think is correct.

Briefly hold up the letter s alphabet card.
Teacher: What letter is this? What sound does it make? Say the sound. Then underline the letter.

1.   d   <u>s</u>   a

Briefly hold up the letter m alphabet card.
Teacher: What letter is this? What sound does it make? Say the sound. Then underline the letter.

2.   p   a   <u>m</u>

Briefly hold up the letter d alphabet card.
Teacher: What letter is this? What sound does it make? Say the sound. Then underline the letter.

3.   <u>d</u>   a   s

Briefly hold up the letter p alphabet card.
Teacher: What letter is this? What sound does it make? Say the sound. Then underline the letter.

4.   <u>p</u>   d   m

Briefly hold up the letter a alphabet card.
Teacher: What letter is this? What sound does it make? Say the sound. Then underline the letter.

5.   p   s   <u>a</u>

Name _____ **Date** _____ **Score** _____

Beginning Sounds

Directions for Teacher: Make a copy of page 90 from the Student Blackline Masters section for each student. Use the student's copy to record results.

Teacher: This activity is about beginning sounds. Listen carefully to what I say. Draw a line under the answer you think is correct.

Teacher: The words are *sit, sun, pan*. Which word begins with a different sound? What sound is it? Say the sound. Then underline the word. *sit, sun, pan*

1.   sit   sun   <u>pan</u>

Teacher: The words are *dog, mud, milk*. Which word begins with a different sound? What sound is it? Say the sound. Then underline the word. *dog, mud, milk*

2.   <u>dog</u>   mud   milk

Teacher: The words are *pass, at, pet*. Which word begins with a different sound? What sound is it? Say the sound. Then underline the word. *pass, at, pet*

3.   pass   <u>at</u>   pet

Teacher: The words are *add, am, sat*. Which word begins with a different sound? What sound is it? Say the sound. Then underline the word. *add, am, sat*

4.   add   am   <u>sat</u>

Teacher: The words are *dig, pat, dot*. Which word begins with a different sound? What sound is it? Say the sound. Then underline the word. *dig, pat, dot*

5.   dig   <u>pat</u>   dot

Assessment

Name _____ Date _____ Score _____

Print Concepts

Directions for Teacher

This assessment may be administered individually using *Pickled Peppers*. As an option, assessment may be based on observations made during regular classroom activities with any available book.

Duplicate page T91 for each student you choose to assess. You will record the student's responses on this page. Sit at a table that allows you and the student to work comfortably. Put the book on the table with the cover down. Ask the questions below and check each question the student answers correctly.

☐ Show me the front cover of this book.

☐ Show me the back cover of this book.

☐ If you were going to read this book, how would you hold it?

(For the following three items, be sure the cover of the book or the title page is showing.)

☐ Point to the title of the book.

☐ Show me the name of the person who wrote the book, the author.

☐ Now show me the name of the person who drew the pictures in the book, the illustrator.

(Turn to the table of contents page.)

☐ Can you tell me what this page is for?

(For the following questions, be sure the student opens the book to a typical two-page spread with an illustration.)

☐ Open the book. Show me a page number.

☐ Point to a word on the page.

☐ How about a letter? Point to a letter for me.

☐ Point to an illustration on the page. An illustration is a picture.

☐ Point to a space between words. How about another space between words?

☐ Run your finger under a sentence. Show me where the sentence begins and ends.

☐ Now point to a space between two sentences. Can you show me another space between two sentences?

☐ If you were reading this page, show me the word you would read first.

☐ Now show me the words you would read next. Move your fingers to show me the direction you would read the words.

☐ After you finish reading the first line on this page, point to the line you would read next and where you would start reading.

☐ If you were reading this page, show me the word you would read last before turning to the next page.

Print Concepts total: _____

Name _____ **Date** _____ **Score** _____

Vocabulary

Directions for Teacher: Make a copy of page 92 from the Student Blackline Masters section for each student. Use the student's copy to record results.

Teacher: Listen carefully to what I say. Draw a line under the answer you think is correct.

Teacher: The word is *predict*. *Predict* means about the same as finish a job. Draw a line under "yes" or "no." *Predict* means about the same as finish a job.

1.   <u>yes</u>   <u>no</u>

Teacher: The word is *temperature*. If you want to know how warm it is outside, you want to know the *temperature*. Draw a line under "yes" or "no." If you want to know how warm it is outside, you want to know the *temperature*.

2.   <u>yes</u>   no

Teacher: The word is *clump*. To *clump* means to carry things carefully. Draw a line under "yes" or "no." To *clump* means to carry things carefully.

3.   yes   <u>no</u>

Teacher: The word is *struggle*. *Struggle* means about the same as freeze. Draw a line under "yes" or "no." *Struggle* means about the same as freeze.

4.   yes   <u>no</u>

Teacher: The word is *report*. A *report* is something that you write or say to other people. Draw a line under "yes" or "no." A *report* is something that you write or say to other people.

5.   <u>yes</u>   no

Teacher: The word is *warn*. To *warn* someone means to give them some food. Draw a line under "yes" or "no." To *warn* someone means to give them some food.

6.   yes   <u>no</u>

Name _____ **Date** _____ **Score** _____

Comprehension

Directions for Teacher: Make a copy of pages 93–94 from the Student Blackline Masters section for each student. Use the student's copy to record results.

Teacher: Look at the pictures for Number 1. Draw a line under the two pictures that go together because they are made of cloth. *Draw a line under the things that are made of cloth.*

1.

Teacher: Move down to Number 2. The picture in the box is a ball. Draw a line under the other picture of something that is like the ball because it is round.

2.

Teacher: Move down to Number 3. The picture in the box is a pen. Draw a line under the other picture of something that is different from the pen because you *cannot* write with it.

3.

Teacher: Now we will do something different. Listen carefully while you look at the pictures. *Reena rode her bike on the rocky trail. She tried to go over a log and lost her balance. She fell into a small stream. She wasn't hurt, but she sure was wet.* Draw a line under the picture that shows what caused Reena to fall.

4.

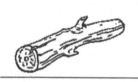      

Teacher: Look at the pictures and listen to this story. *Something had eaten Mrs. Lee's flowers. Then she saw a rabbit on the lawn. She was pretty sure she knew who ate the flowers. She put a fence around her flowers.* Draw a line under the picture that shows the effect of the rabbit eating the flowers.

5.

Name _____ **Date** _____ **Score** _____

Comprehension, Text Features, and Story Elements

Directions for Teacher: Look at the images and listen to this question. *Which picture would go best with a story about fixing a leaky faucet?* Draw a line under the image that would go best with a story about fixing a leaky faucet?

6.

Teacher: Listen to this sentence from a story. *Jacob gave Suki a book for her birthday.* Would a picture of a girl opening a gift go with this story? If it would, draw a line under "yes." If it would not, draw a line under "no." *Jacob gave Suki a book for her birthday.* Would a picture of a girl opening a gift go with this story? Draw a line under "yes" or "no." Would a picture of a girl opening a gift go with this story?

7. <u>yes</u>   no

Teacher: Look at the pictures and listen to this story. *The chair was beside the window. Pat moved it close to the door. He changed his mind and put the chair near the fireplace.* Draw a line under the picture that shows what happened last in this story.

8.

Teacher: Listen to this story. *The mouse put on her coat and went outside. A harsh wind whipped her face. Snowflakes stuck to her paws. She slammed the door and went to the kitchen to make some tea.* Is it summer in this story? Draw a line under "yes" or "no." Is it summer?

9. yes   <u>no</u>

Teacher: Listen to this story. *Jasmine could not wait to show her dad what she had learned. She slipped into the pool. She swam all the way to the other side!* Does Jasmine want to show her dad something new she learned? Draw a line under "yes" or "no." Does Jasmine want to show her dad something new she learned?

10. <u>yes</u>   no

Name _____ **Date** _____ **Score** _____

Grammar, Usage, and Mechanics

Directions for Teacher: Make a copy of page 95 from the Student Blackline Masters section for each student. Use the student's copy to record results.

Teacher: Listen to the sentence for Number 1 as I read it out loud. *Was the fresh pineapple sweet?* Should this sentence end with a period because it is declarative? Draw a line under "yes" or "no." *Was the fresh pineapple sweet?*

1. yes   <u>no</u>

Teacher: Listen to the sentence for Number 2 as I read it out loud. *Our ride was smooth.* Should this sentence end with a period because it is declarative? Draw a line under "yes" or "no." *Our ride was smooth.*

2. <u>yes</u>   no

Teacher: Declarative sentences begin with a capital letter and end with a period. Look at the sentence for Number 3 while I read it out loud. *Insects have six legs.* If the sentence begins with a capital letter and ends with a period, underline "yes." If not, underline "no." Does the sentence begin with a capital letter and end with a period? *Yes* or *no.*

3. Insects have six legs.

<u>yes</u>   no

Teacher: Look at the sentence for Number 4 while I read it out loud. *Water freezes when it gets cold.* If the sentence begins with a capital letter and ends with a period, underline "yes." If not, underline "no." Does the sentence begin with a capital letter and end with a period? *Yes* or *no.*

4. water freezes when it gets cold.

yes   <u>no</u>

Teacher: Look at the sentence for Number 5 while I read it out loud. *A baby frog is a tadpole.* If the sentence begins with a capital letter and ends with a period, underline "yes." If not, underline "no." Does the sentence begin with a capital letter and end with a period? *Yes* or *no.*

5. A baby frog is a tadpole

yes   <u>no</u>

Name _____ **Date** _____ **Score** _____

Blending Initial Sounds

Directions for Teacher: Duplicate page T96 for each student you choose to assess. Record results on this page.

Teacher: Put these word parts together and tell me the word. Are you ready?/h/ (pause for two seconds) *ut*

1. ☐ hut

Teacher: Put these word parts together and tell me the word. Are you ready?/m/ (pause for two seconds) *iss*

2. ☐ miss

Teacher: Put these word parts together and tell me the word. Are you ready?/h/ (pause for two seconds) *oop*

3. ☐ hoop

Teacher: Put these word parts together and tell me the word. Are you ready?/d/ (pause for two seconds) *ive*

4. ☐ dive

Teacher: Put these word parts together and tell me the word. Are you ready?/p/ (pause for two seconds) *eel*

5. ☐ peel

Assessment

Name _____   Date _____   Score _____

Blending Final Sounds

Directions for Teacher: Duplicate page T97 for each student you choose to assess. Record results on this page.

Teacher: Put these word parts together and tell me the word. Are you ready? *fla* (pause for two seconds) /t/

1. ☐ flat

Teacher: Put these word parts together and tell me the word. Are you ready? *thi* (pause for two seconds) /s/

2. ☐ this

Teacher: Put these word parts together and tell me the word. Are you ready? *san* (pause for two seconds) /d/

3. ☐ sand

Teacher: Put these word parts together and tell me the word. Are you ready? *ne* (pause for two seconds) /t/

4. ☐ net

Teacher: Put these word parts together and tell me the word. Are you ready? *sli* (pause for two seconds) /p/

5. ☐ slip

Selection Vocabulary

Directions for Teacher: Make a copy of page 98 from the Student Blackline Masters section for each student. Use the student's copy to record results.

Teacher: Listen carefully to what I say. Draw a line under the answer you think is correct.

Teacher: Which picture shows a *driver*? Draw a line under the picture that shows a *driver*.

1.

Teacher: Which of these has a *horn* that makes a noise? Draw a line under the picture that shows something with a *horn* that makes noise.

2.

Teacher: Which door is *shut*? Draw a line under the picture that shows the door that is *shut*.

3.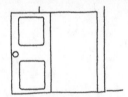

Teacher: Which picture shows a *town*? Draw a line under the picture that shows a *town*.

4.

Teacher: Which picture shows something with *wipers*? Draw a line under the picture that shows something with *wipers*.

5.

Name _____ **Date** _____ **Score** _____

Main Idea and Details

Directions for Teacher: Make a copy of page 99 from the Student Blackline Masters section for each student. Use the student's copy to record results.

Teacher: Look at the pictures and listen to this story. *Wolves live in places like mountains and forests. They hunt other animals for food. Wolves live in a group called a pack.* Draw a line under the picture that shows what this story is mostly about.

1.

Teacher: Look at the pictures and listen to this story. *Long ago, people made pens out of feathers. They dipped the tip of the feather in ink.* Then they wrote on paper or other things. Draw a line under the picture that shows what pens were made of long ago.

2.

Genre Knowledge

Teacher: In this activity, you will decide if the story is a nursery rhyme or not. Listen to the story I read. Draw a line under "yes" if the story is a nursery rhyme. Draw a line under "no" if it is not. Are you ready?

Teacher: *Tick-tock goes the clock and wakes me up in the morning.* If this is a nursery rhyme, draw a line under "yes." If it is not, draw a line under "no." *Tick-tock goes the clock and wakes me up in the morning.*

1.   yes   no

Teacher: *"Buzz, buzz," goes the bee. If I close my eyes, it won't sting me.* If this is a nursery rhyme, draw a line under "yes." If it is not, draw a line under "no." *"Buzz, buzz," goes the bee. If I close my eyes, it won't sting me.*

2.   yes   no

Name _____ **Date** _____ **Score** _____

Grammar, Usage, and Mechanics

Directions for Teacher: Make a copy of page 100 from the Student Blackline Masters section for each student. Use the student's copy to record results.

Teacher: You learned before about interrogative sentences. These sentences ask questions, not give information. This activity is about sentences that ask questions.

Teacher: Listen to this sentence. If it is an interrogative sentence and asks a question, draw a line under "yes." If it is not, draw a line under "no." *Seals are animals that live in the ocean.* Does this sentence ask a question? Draw a line under "yes" or "no." *Seals are animals that live in the ocean.*

1. yes   <u>no</u>

Teacher: Listen to this sentence. If it is an interrogative sentence and asks a question, draw a line under "yes." If it is not, draw a line under "no." *How far away is the moon?* Does this sentence ask a question? Draw a line under "yes" or "no." *How far away is the moon?*

2. <u>yes</u>   no

Teacher: Listen to this sentence. If it is an interrogative sentence and asks a question, draw a line under "yes." If it is not, draw a line under "no." *How many days are in a year?* Does this sentence ask a question? Draw a line under "yes" or "no." *How many days are in a year?*

3. <u>yes</u>   no

Teacher: Listen to this sentence. If it is an interrogative sentence and asks a question, draw a line under "yes." If it is not, draw a line under "no." *A dog's foot is called a paw.* Does this sentence ask a question? Draw a line under "yes" or "no." *A dog's foot is called a paw.*

4. yes   <u>no</u>

Teacher: Listen to this sentence. If it is an interrogative sentence and asks a question, draw a line under "yes." If it is not, draw a line under "no." *Where do eagles live?* Does this sentence ask a question? Draw a line under "yes" or "no." *Where do eagles live?*

5. <u>yes</u>   no

Name _____ **Date** _____ **Score** _____

Letter Sounds

Directions for Teacher: Make a copy of page 101 from the Student Blackline Masters section for each student. Use the student's copy to record results.

Teacher: This activity is about letter sounds. Listen carefully to what I say. Draw a line under the letter you think is correct.

Teacher: The word in the box should be *hat*. Which letter should go at the beginning of the word *hat*? What sound does it make?

1. 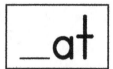   m   p

Teacher: The word in the box should be *let*. Which letter should go at the beginning of the word *let*? What sound does it make?

2. 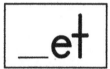   s   n   <u>l</u>

Teacher: The word in the box should be *nap*. Which letter should go at the beginning of the word *nap*? What sound does it make?

3. 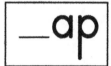   <u>n</u>   c   m

Teacher: The word in the box should be *but*. Which letter should go at the end of the word *but*? What sound does it make?

4.    s   n

Teacher: The word in the box should be *hen*. Which letter should go at the end of the word *hen*? What sound does it make?

5.    <u>n</u>   d   s

Assessment

Name _____ Date _____ Score _____

Phoneme Manipulation:
Initial Sounds

Directions for Teacher: Duplicate page T102 for each student you choose to assess. Record results on this page.

Teacher: Listen to this word: *and*. If you change the first sound to /e/, what new word do you have? The word is *and*; change the first sound to /e/.

1. ☐ end

Teacher: Listen to this word: *nut*. If you change the first sound to /b/, what new word do you have? The word is *nut*; change the first sound to /b/.

2. ☐ but

Teacher: Listen to this word: *mad*. If you change the first sound to /s/, what new word do you have? The word is *mad*; change the first sound to /s/.

3. ☐ sad

Teacher: Listen to this word: *red*. If you change the first sound to /f/, what new word do you have? The word is *red*; change the first sound to /f/.

4. ☐ fed

Teacher: Listen to this word: *call*. If you change the first sound to /h/, what new word do you have? The word is *call*; change the first sound to /h/.

5. ☐ hall

Name _____ **Date** _____ **Score** _____

Selection Vocabulary

Directions for Teacher: Make a copy of page 103 from the Student Blackline Masters section for each student. Use the student's copy to record results.

Teacher: Listen carefully to what I say. Draw a line under the answer you think is correct.

Teacher: Which picture shows a *dump truck*? Draw a line under the picture that shows a *dump truck*.

1.

Teacher: Which picture shows something that might bring good *luck*? Draw a line under the picture that shows something that might bring good *luck*.

2.

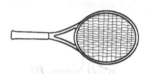  

Teacher: Which picture shows someone *pulling*? Draw a line under the picture that shows someone *pulling*.

3.

Teacher: Which picture shows a *shopping cart*? Draw a line under the picture that shows a *shopping cart*.

4.

Teacher: A *puff* of air will blow out a candle. Underline "yes" or "no." A *puff* of air will blow out a candle.

5.   yes   no

Sequence

Directions for Teacher: Make a copy of page 104 from the Student Blackline Masters section for each student. Use the student's copy to record results.

Teacher: This activity is about sequencing. Listen to each story I read. Pay attention to the order of things in the story. Listen to the question. Draw a line under the picture that shows the best answer to each question.

Teacher: *Julie rode her bike to the store. She bought some things and then got on her bike. She rode to her grandfather's house. She sat on the porch with him for a while.* Draw a line under the thing that happened last in this story.

1.

Teacher: *The duck sat on her nest. After a few weeks, her eggs hatched. Before long, her babies were swimming in the pond with her.* Draw a line under the thing that happened first in this story.

2.

Text Features

Teacher: In this activity, you will answer questions about poetry.

Teacher: Listen to this sentence for Number 1. Listen carefully. *A stanza is a picture that tells about a poem.* If this is true, draw a line under "yes." If it is not true, draw a line under "no." *A stanza is a picture that tells about a poem.*

1. <u>yes</u>　　　<u>no</u>

Teacher: Move down to Number 2. Listen carefully to this question. *Is a stanza part of a poem?* Draw a line under "yes" or "no." *Is a stanza part of a poem?*

2. <u>yes</u>　　　no

Name _____ Date _____ Score _____

Grammar, Usage, and Mechanics

Directions for Teacher: Make a copy of page 105 from the Student Blackline Masters section for each student. Use the student's copy to record results.

Teacher: In this activity, we will work with sentences. Listen carefully to what I say because we will be doing different things.

Teacher: Look at Number 1. Listen to what I say and look at what is in the box. You must decide if it is a word or a sentence. *A bird has feathers.* If this is a sentence, draw a line under "yes." If not, draw a line under "no." Is what is in the box a sentence? Yes or no.

1. | A bird has feathers. | <u>yes</u> no

Teacher: Move down to Number 2. Listen to what I say and look at what is in the box. You must decide if it is a word or a sentence. *Ceiling.* If this is a word, draw a line under "yes." If not, draw a line under "no." Is what is in the box a word? Yes or no.

2. | ceiling | <u>yes</u> no

Teacher: Look at Number 3. Listen to what I say and look at what is in the box. You must decide if it is a word or a sentence. *Basement.* If this is a sentence, draw a line under "yes." If not, draw a line under "no." Is what is in the box a sentence? Yes or no.

3. | basement | yes <u>no</u>

Teacher: Now we will do something different. You already learned about sentences that ask a question. Listen to this sentence. Decide what end mark it needs. Does it need a period, an exclamation point, or a question mark? *Is a chipmunk an animal?* Draw a line under the punctuation it needs. *Is a chipmunk an animal?*

4. . <u>?</u> !

Teacher: Listen to this sentence. Decide what end mark it needs. Does it need a period, an exclamation point, or a question mark? *When did Alaska become a state?* Draw a line under the punctuation it needs. *When did Alaska become a state?*

5. . <u>?</u> !

Assessment

Name _____ **Date** _____ **Score** _____

Short-Vowel Sounds

Directions for Teacher: Make a copy of page 106 from the Student Blackline Masters section for each student. Use the student's copy to record results.

Teacher: This activity is about short-vowel sounds. Listen carefully to what I say. Draw a line under the letter you think is correct.

Teacher: The word in the box should be *pat*. Which letter should go in the middle of the word *pat*?

1.   a   i

Teacher: The word in the box should be *hid*. Which letter should go in the middle of the word *hid*?

2.   a   i

Teacher: The word in the box should be *it*. Which letter should go in the beginning of the word *it*?

3.   a   i

Teacher: The word in the box should be *ran*. Which letter should go in the middle of the word *ran*?

4.   a   i

Teacher: The word in the box should be *lip*. Which letter should go in the middle of the word *lip*?

5.   a   i

Name _____ Date _____ Score _____

High-Frequency Words

Directions for Teacher: Make a copy of page 107 from the Student Blackline Masters section for each student. Use the student's copy to record results.

Teacher: This activity is about words you have learned. Listen carefully to what I say. Draw a line under the word you think is correct.

Teacher: The word is *have. They have a truck.* Draw a line under *have.*

1. had   has   <u>have</u>

Teacher: The word is *as. The floor is as cold as ice.* Draw a line under *as.*

2. <u>as</u>   to   it

Teacher: The word is *it. Have you seen it?* Draw a line under *it.*

3. <u>it</u>   am   is

Teacher: The word is *to. Hand the pen to me.* Draw a line under *to.*

4. go   <u>to</u>   you

Teacher: The word is *at. We will leave at noon.* Draw a line under *at.*

5. in   a   <u>at</u>

Name _____ **Date** _____ **Score** ____

High-Frequency Words

Directions for Teacher: Make a copy of page 108 from the Student Blackline Masters section for each student. Use the student's copy to record results.

Teacher: This activity is about reading words. Look at these words. Read them to me one at a time, starting on the left.

had   in   the   is   and

Scoring:

☐ had   ☐ in   ☐ the   ☐ is   ☐ and   Total: ___

☐ Student read words at a pace that suggests they were recognized automatically.

Name _____ **Date** _____ **Score** _____

Segmenting: Onset and Rime

Directions for Teacher: Duplicate page T109 for each student you choose to assess. Record results on this page.

Teacher: I will say a word. I want you to say the same word, but break it into two parts. Here is what I mean. The word is *fun*. The two parts are /f/ *un*. Now you try it. Say the word *fun* in two parts.

Teacher: The word is *ball*. Say the word *ball* in two parts.

1. ☐ /b/ all

Teacher: The word is *wish*. Say the word *wish* in two parts.

2. ☐ /w/ ish

Teacher: The word is *dog*. Say the word *dog* in two parts.

3. ☐ /d/ og

Teacher: The word is *get*. Say the word *get* in two parts.

4. ☐ /g/ et

Teacher: The word is *run*. Say the word *run* in two parts.

5. ☐ /r/ un

Name _____ **Date** _____ **Score** _____

Selection Vocabulary

Directions for Teacher: Make a copy of page 110 from the Student Blackline Masters section for each student. Use the student's copy to record results.

Teacher: Listen carefully to what I say. Draw a line under the answer you think is correct.

Teacher: Which picture shows a *loop*? Draw a line under the picture that shows a *loop*.

1.

Teacher: Which picture shows something that is *circular*? Draw a line under the picture that shows something that is *circular*.

2.

Teacher: Which picture shows a place with *rides*? Draw a line under the picture that shows a place with *rides*.

3.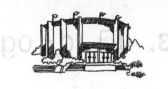

Teacher: Which picture shows *tracks*? Draw a line under the picture that shows *tracks*.

4.

Teacher: A *great* story is one that you like. Underline "yes" or "no." A *great* story is one that you like.

5. yes   no

Assessment

Name _____ Date _____ Score _____

Cause and Effect

Directions for Teacher: Make a copy of page 111 from the Student Blackline Masters section for each student. Use the student's copy to record results.

Teacher: This activity is about cause and effect, things you learned about before. Listen carefully to the story and question before choosing your answer.

Teacher: Listen to the story for Number 1. *The car was stuck in the mud. A tow truck came and pulled the car out of the mud. The car was dirty, but the driver was okay.* Draw a line under the picture that shows what caused the car to be pulled out of the mud.

1.

Teacher: Move down to Number 2. Listen carefully and look at the pictures. *Mr. Chan was cleaning the house. He turned on the vacuum cleaner. The dog and cat ran into the kitchen. They did not like the sound.* Draw a line under the picture that shows what caused the dog and cat to run into the kitchen.

2.

Story Elements

Teacher: This activity is about the characters and setting in stories. These are the people or animals in the story and the place the story happens.

Teacher: Listen carefully and look at the pictures for Number 1. *A bird landed on the roof of the house. A dog played in the yard, and the cat sat on the deck. Alice took a picture of all the animals.* Draw a line under the character who sat on the deck.

1.

Teacher: Move down to Number 2. *The swimming pool was crowded for the big meet. Students from all the schools in the area would compete. It was a warm, sunny day that was perfect for the event.* Draw a line under the picture that shows where this story takes place.

2.

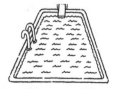  

Name _____ **Date** _____ **Score** _____

Grammar, Usage, and Mechanics

Directions for Teacher: Make a copy of page 112 from the Student Blackline Masters section for each student. Use the student's copy to record results.

Teacher: In this activity, you will listen for expanded sentences. The sentences will be questions, and you will decide if they make sense. I will read a sentence and then expand it. You will underline "yes" if the sentence makes sense and "no" if it does not.

Teacher: Listen carefully to the first sentence. *What time will you go?* Now listen to the expanded sentence. *What time will you go to the store?* Is the expanded sentence correct? Underline "yes" or "no." *What time will you go to the store?*

1.   yes   no

Teacher: Listen to the first sentence for Number 2. *Did you see her?* Now listen to the expanded sentence. *Did you see the friend her?* Is the expanded sentence correct? Underline "yes" or "no." *Did you see the friend her?*

2.   yes   <u>no</u>

Teacher: Listen to the first sentence for Number 3. *Where is the flower?* Now listen to the expanded sentence. *Where is the flower ready now?* Is the expanded sentence correct? Underline "yes" or "no." *Where is the flower ready now?*

3.   yes   <u>no</u>

Teacher: Listen to the first sentence for Number 4. *Can someone fix this?* Now listen to the expanded sentence. *Can someone fix this flat tire?* Is the expanded sentence correct? Underline "yes" or "no." *Can someone fix this flat tire?*

4.   yes   no

Teacher: Listen to the first sentence for Number 5. *Will it rain tomorrow?* Now listen to the expanded sentence. *Will it rain tomorrow and the cloud?* Is the expanded sentence correct? Underline "yes" or "no." *Will it rain tomorrow and the cloud?*

5.   yes   <u>no</u>

Name _____ **Date** _____ **Score** _____

Letters and Sounds

Directions for Teacher: Make a copy of page 113 from the Student Blackline Masters section for each student. Use the student's copy to record results.

Teacher: This activity is about the sounds that letters make. Listen carefully to what I say. Draw a line under the answer you think is correct.

Hold up the letter *h* alphabet card.

Teacher: What letter is this? What sound does it make? Say the sound. Then underline the letter.

1.　　m　　　　h　　　　i

Hold up the letter *t* alphabet card.
Teacher: What letter is this? What sound does it make? Say the sound. Then underline the letter.

2.　　t　　　　g　　　　h

Hold up the letter *n* alphabet card.
Teacher: What letter is this? What sound does it make? Say the sound. Then underline the letter.

3.　　s　　　　m　　　　n

Hold up the letter *l* alphabet card.
Teacher: What letter is this? What sound does it make? Say the sound. Then underline the letter.

4.　　h　　　　n　　　　l

Hold up the letter *i* alphabet card.
Teacher: What letter is this? What sound does it make? Say the sound. Then underline the letter.

5.　　i　　　　l　　　　a

Name _____ Date _____ Score _____

Ending Sounds

Directions for Teacher: Duplicate page T114 for each student you choose to assess. Record results on this page.

Teacher: Listen to these words: *at on it*. Which word ends with a different sound? What sound is it? *at on it*

1. ☐ on   ☐ /n/

Teacher: Listen to these words: *hill red sad*. Which word ends with a different sound? What sound is it? *hill red sad*

2. ☐ hill   ☐ /l/

Teacher: Listen to these words: *let lip sat*. Which two words end with the same sound? What sound is it? *let lip sat*

3. ☐ let, sat   ☐ /t/

Teacher: Listen to these words: *or store bus*. Which word ends with a different sound? What sound is it? *or store bus*

4. ☐ bus   ☐ /s/

Teacher: Listen to these words: *him have them*. Which two words end with the same sound? What sound is it? *him have them*

5. ☐ him, them   ☐ /m/

Name _____ **Date** _____ **Score** _____

Segmenting: Onset and Rime

Directions for Teacher: Duplicate page T115 for each student you choose to assess. Record results on this page.

Teacher: I will say a word. I want you to say the same word, but break it into two parts. Here is what I mean. The word is *fun*. The two parts are /f/ *un*. Now you try it. Say the word *fun* in two parts.

Teacher: The word is *down*. Say the word *down* in two parts.

1. ☐ /d/ own

Teacher: The word is *help*. Say the word *help* in two parts.

2. ☐ /h/ elp

Teacher: The word is *toy*. Say the word *toy* in two parts.

3. ☐ /t/ oy

Teacher: The word is *with*. Say the word *with* in two parts.

4. ☐ /w/ ith

Teacher: The word is *bark*. Say the word *bark* in two parts.

5. ☐ /b/ ark

UNIT 4 • Assessment (continued)

Name _____ **Date** _____ **Score** _____

Vocabulary

Directions for Teacher: Make a copy of page 116 from the Student Blackline Masters section for each student. Use the student's copy to record results.

Teacher: Listen carefully to what I say. Draw a line under the answer you think is correct.

Teacher: The word is *through*. You can walk *through* a building to get out the other side. Draw a line under "yes" or "no." You can walk *through* a building to get out the other side.

1. yes   no

Teacher: The word is *wheels*. Most cars have four wheels. Draw a line under "yes" or "no." Most cars have four *wheels*.

2. yes   no

Teacher: The word is *luck*. When you have good *luck*, nice things happen. Draw a line under "yes" or "no." When you have good *luck*, nice things happen.

3. yes   no

Teacher: The word is *surprise*. A *surprise* is a kind of food. Draw a line under "yes" or "no." A *surprise* is a kind of food.

4. yes   no

Teacher: The word is *opposite*. *Opposite* is another name for confused. Draw a line under "yes" or "no." *Opposite* is another name for confused.

5. yes   no

Teacher: The word is *round*. Going *round* in a boat means it is sinking. Draw a line under "yes" or "no." Going *round* in a boat means it is sinking.

6. yes   no

Copyright © McGraw Hill. Permission is granted to reproduce for classroom use.

Assessment

Name _____ **Date** _____ **Score** _____

Comprehension

Directions for Teacher: Make a copy of pages 117–118 from the Student Blackline Masters section for each student. Use the student's copy to record results.

Teacher: In this activity, you will answer different kinds of questions. Listen carefully to what I say so you will know what to do.

Teacher: Look at the pictures for Number 1 and listen to this story. *Vincent was an artist. He painted people, the sky, trees, and cities. His paintings were very pretty.* Draw a line under the picture that shows what this story is mostly about.

1.

Teacher: Look at the pictures for Number 2 and listen to this story. *Maddie's room is really nice. She has a big window. The walls are covered with posters and pictures. Maddie's favorite thing in the room is a wooden box her grandfather made.* Draw a line under the picture that shows what Maddie likes best in her room.

2.

Teacher: Look at the pictures for Number 3 and listen to this story. *The bee landed on the flower. It tasted the sweet nectar. Then the bee flew back to its nest. The bee did a dance that told the others about the flowers.* Draw a line under the thing that happened first in this story.

3.

Teacher: Move down to Number 4. *The water was a little choppy. The motorboat went slowly back to the dock, but it bumped a rock. The rock made a hole in the boat, and some water got into the boat. The man used a bucket to get the water out until the boat reached the dock.* Draw a line under the picture that shows what caused the hole in the boat.

4.

Teacher: Look at the pictures for Number 5. Listen to this story. *The mountains were very high. A stream flowed down the mountains. It ran over rocks and logs. The stream moved very quickly and cut a deep canyon in the ground.* Draw a line under the picture that shows the effect of the moving water.

5.

Name _____ **Date** _____ **Score** _____

Comprehension

Teacher: For Number 6, you will listen to what I say. If it is a nursery rhyme, draw a line under "yes." If not, draw a line under "no." Listen carefully. *The little puppy could not wait and rushed right through the garden gate.* Draw a line under "yes" if this is a nursery rhyme or "no" if it is not. *The little puppy could not wait and rushed right through the garden gate.*

6. <u>yes</u>   no

Teacher: Listen to what I say. If it is a nursery rhyme, draw a line under "yes." If not, draw a line under "no." Listen carefully. *The sun peaks out over the hill. It's time to get up, but I'm sleeping still!* Draw a line under "yes" if this is a nursery rhyme or "no" if it is not. *The sun peaks out over the hill. It's time to get up, but I'm sleeping still!*

7. <u>yes</u>   no

Teacher: Move down to Number 8. Listen to what I say. *A poem has four groups or sets of lines. This means the poem has four stanzas.* Draw a line under "yes" if this is true or "no" if it is not. *A poem that has four sets of lines has four stanzas.* Draw a line under "yes" or "no."

8. <u>yes</u>   no

Teacher: For Number 9, listen to this stanza of a poem. Each line will end with a rhyming word. Draw a line under the answer that tells how many lines are in the stanza.
Look over there into the sky
To see the flocks of birds go by.

9. 1   <u>2</u>   3

Teacher: Look at the pictures for Number 10 and listen to this story. *The bear stood beside the river. A hawk flew over the river, and a bobcat wandered through the woods not far away.* Draw a line under the picture of the animal in the story who stood beside the river.

10.    

Assessment

Name _____ **Date** _____ **Score** _____

Grammar, Usage, and Mechanics

Directions for Teacher: Make a copy of page 119 from the Student Blackline Masters section for each student. Use the student's copy to record results.

Teacher: Look at Number 1. There are two answers. One is a sentence and one is a word. Draw a line under the sentence...under the sentence.

1. garage   <u>The light is on.</u>

Teacher: Look at Number 2. There are two answers. One is a sentence and one is a word. Draw a line under the word...under the word.

2. This is my hat.   <u>shovel</u>

Teacher: Move down to Number 3. Look at the sentence as I read it out loud. *How far away is the moon?* Should this sentence end with a question mark? Underline "yes" or "no." *How far away is the moon?*

3. How far away is the moon

<u>yes</u>   no

Teacher: Move down to Number 4. I will read two sentences. You will tell me if the second one is correct. Listen carefully to the first sentence. *Where is the coat?* Now listen to the expanded sentence. *Where is the coat to be red?* Is the expanded sentence correct? Underline "yes" or "no." *Where is the coat to be red?*

4. yes   <u>no</u>

Teacher: Move down to Number 5. I will read two sentences. You will tell me if the second one is correct. Listen carefully to the first sentence. *Are you going home?* Now listen to the expanded sentence. *Are you going home now or later?* Is the expanded sentence correct? Underline "yes" or "no." *Are you going home now or later?*

5. <u>yes</u>   no

Name _____ Date _____ Score ____

Letter Sounds

Directions for Teacher: Duplicate page T120 for each student you choose to assess. Record results on this page.

Teacher: Listen to this word: *cat*. When you spell *cat*, what letter comes first? What sound does it make?

1. ☐ c   ☐ /k/

Teacher: Listen to this word: *bed*. When you spell *bed*, what letter comes first? What sound does it make?

2. ☐ b   ☐ /b/

Teacher: Listen to this word: *rub*. When you spell *rub*, what letter comes last? What sound does it make?

3. ☐ b   ☐ /b/

Teacher: Listen to this word: *cold*. When you spell *cold*, what letter comes first? What sound does it make?

4. ☐ c   ☐ /k/

Teacher: Listen to this word: *crab*. When you spell *crab*, what letter comes last? What sound does it make?

5. ☐ b   ☐ /b/

Assessment

Name _____ Date _____ Score _____

Phoneme Segmentation

Directions for Teacher: Duplicate page T121 for each student you choose to assess. Record results on this page.

Teacher: I will say all the sounds in a word. I want you to count the sounds. You can count 1-2-3, or you can hold up a finger for each sound you hear. I will show you what I mean. The word is /f/ /u/ /n/. See how I held up a finger for each sound? There are three sounds in /f/ /u/ /n/.

Teacher: The word is /b/ /i/ /g/. How many sounds do you hear in /b/ /i/ /g/? Hold up a finger or count each sound in /b/ /i/ /g/.

1. ☐ 3

Teacher: The word is /i/ /f/. How many sounds do you hear in /i/ /f/? Hold up a finger or count each sound in /i/ /f/.

2. ☐ 2

Teacher: The word is /l/ /o/ /t/. Hold up a finger or count each sound in /l/ /o/ /t/.

3. ☐ 3

Teacher: The word is /u/ /p/. Hold up a finger or count each sound in /u/ /p/.

4. ☐ 2

Teacher: The word is /s/ /l/ /e/ /d/. Hold up a finger or count each sound in /s/ /l/ /e/ /d/.

5. ☐ 4

Name _____ **Date** _____ **Score** _____

Selection Vocabulary

Directions for Teacher: Make a copy of page 122 from the Student Blackline Masters section for each student. Use the student's copy to record results.

Teacher: Listen carefully to what I say. Draw a line under the answer you think is correct.

Teacher: Which picture shows a *cabin*? Draw a line under the picture that shows a *cabin*.

1.

Teacher: Which picture shows the most *space* between things? Draw a line under the picture that shows the most *space* between things.

2.

Teacher: Which picture shows *stilts*? Draw a line under the picture that shows *stilts*.

3.

Teacher: Which picture shows something that is *sturdy*? Draw a line under the picture that shows something that is *sturdy*.

4.

Teacher: Which picture shows a way to *welcome* people? Draw a line under the picture that shows a way to *welcome* people.

5.

Assessment

Name _____ Date _____ Score _____

Classify and Categorize

Directions for Teacher: Make a copy of page 123 from the Student Blackline Masters section for each student. Use the student's copy to record results.

Teacher: In this activity, you will group things together because they are alike.

Teacher: Look at the pictures for Number 1. Draw a line under the two pictures that go together because they show *things that help you go up...things that help you go up.*

1.

Teacher: Look at the pictures for Number 2. Draw a line under the two pictures that go together because they are *shapes that only have straight lines...shapes that only have straight lines.*

2.

Text Features and Language Use

Teacher: In this activity, you will match pictures and captions. You learned before that captions are words that tell something about pictures. You will also answer questions about exclamatory sentences. These sentences show emotions.

Teacher: Look at the picture for Number 1. Listen to this caption. *The sun is the star nearest Earth.* Draw a line under "yes" or "no." Do the words match the picture? *The sun is the star nearest Earth.*

1.
        <u>yes</u>   <u>no</u>

Teacher: Number 2 is different. Listen to this sentence. Think about what kind of punctuation mark it needs. *Don't move or the bee will sting you!* Draw a line under the correct end mark. *Don't move or the bee will sting you!*

2.   **?**   <u>!</u>

Assessment

Name _____ **Date** _____ **Score** _____

Grammar, Usage, and Mechanics

Directions for Teacher: Make a copy of page 124 from the Student Blackline Masters section for each student. Use the student's copy to record results.

Teacher: In this activity, you will answer questions about exclamatory sentences. You learned before that exclamatory sentences show emotion.

Teacher: Listen to this sentence for Number 1. If it is an exclamatory sentence, draw a line under "yes." If it is not, draw a line under "no." *Watch out for that hole in the ground!* Is this an exclamatory sentence? Draw a line under "yes" or "no." *Watch out for that hole in the ground!*

1. yes   no

Teacher: Move down to Number 2. Listen carefully to this sentence. *A woodpecker is a kind of bird.* Is this an exclamatory sentence? Draw a line under "yes" or "no." *A woodpecker is a kind of bird.*

2. yes   no

Teacher: Look at the sentence for Number 3 as I read it out loud. *What is the name of that star?* Should this sentence end with an exclamation point? Draw a line under "yes" or "no." *What is the name of that star?*

3. What is the name of that star

      yes   no

Teacher: Move down to Number 4. Listen carefully as I read the sentence. *Wow, that is a great story you wrote!* Should this sentence end with an exclamation point?

4. Wow, that is a great story you wrote

      yes   no

Teacher: Look at the sentence for Number 5. Listen carefully as I read the sentence. *That cloud is a nimbus cloud.* Should this sentence end with an exclamation point?

5. That cloud is a nimbus cloud

      yes   no

Assessment

Name _____ **Date** _____ **Score** _____

Letter Sounds

Directions for Teacher: Duplicate page T125 for each student you choose to assess. Record results on this page.

Teacher: Listen to this word: *hot*. When you spell *hot*, what letter comes in the middle? What sound does it make?

1. ☐ o ☐ /o/

Teacher: Listen to this word: *rain*. When you spell *rain*, what letter comes first? What sound does it make?

2. ☐ r ☐ /r/

Teacher: Listen to this word: *her*. When you spell *her*, what letter comes last? What sound does it make?

3. ☐ r ☐ /r/

Teacher: Listen to this word: *doll*. When you spell *doll*, what letter comes second? Whar sound does it make?

4. ☐ o ☐ /o/

Teacher: Listen to this word: *fur*. When you spell *fur*, what letter comes last? What sound does it make?

5. ☐ r ☐ /r/

Name _____ **Date** _____ **Score** _____

Phoneme Matching: Initial and Final Sounds

Directions for Teacher: Duplicate page T126 for each student you choose to assess. Record results on this page.

Teacher: Listen to these words: *bend hand bus*. Which two words begin with the same sound? *bend hand bus*

1. ☐ bend, bus

Teacher: Listen to these words: *desk call comb*. Which two words begin with the same sound? *desk call comb*

2. ☐ call, comb

Teacher: Listen to these words: *rub cab hut*. Which two words end with the same sound? *rub cab hut*

3. ☐ rub, cab

Teacher: Listen to these words: *team reach roll*. Which two words begin with the same sound? *team reach roll*

4. ☐ reach, roll

Teacher: Listen to these words: *hair late store*. Which two words end with the same sound? *hair late store*

5. ☐ hair, store

Assessment

Name _____   **Date** _____   **Score** _____

Selection Vocabulary

Directions for Teacher: Make a copy of page 127 from the Student Blackline Masters section for each student. Use the student's copy to record results.

Teacher: Listen carefully to what I say. Draw a line under the answer you think is correct.

Teacher: Which picture shows *grain*? Draw a line under the picture that shows *grain*.

1.

Teacher: Does *polluted* mean clean or dirty? Draw a line under your answer. Does *polluted* mean clean or dirty?

2.

Teacher: Which picture shows someone who *provides* water? Draw a line under the picture that shows someone who *provides* water.

3.

Teacher: Which picture shows someone who is going to *replace* a light bulb? Draw a line under the picture that shows someone who is going to *replace* a light bulb.

4.

Teacher: Which picture shows a person close to a *base*? Draw a line under the picture that shows a person close to a *base*.

5.

Name _____ Date _____ Score _____

Main Idea and Details

Directions for Teacher: Make a copy of page 128 from the Student Blackline Masters section for each student. Use the student's copy to record results.

Teacher: For this activity, you will listen to stories and answer questions about them.

Teacher: Look at the pictures for Number 1 and listen to this story. *The chipmunk nibbled some seeds that were on the ground. It took a drink from the stream and then went back to its burrow under some rocks.* Draw a line under the picture that shows what the chipmunk ate.

1.

Teacher: Move down to Number 2. Listen carefully. *The two friends were paddling a canoe. They went out into the lake to a small island. The paddled around the island and then came back to the dock.* Draw a line under the picture that shows what kind of boat the friends used.

2.

Language Use

Teacher: You will do different kinds of things in this activity. Listen carefully and think about what I say.

Teacher: Look at the answers for Number 1. You learned about imperative sentences before. These sentences give a command. Listen to this sentence. It is an imperative sentence and gives a command. *Stir the flour into the batter.* Underline the correct end mark. *Stir the flour into the batter.*

1.

Teacher: Move down to Number 2. Listen to the sentence. If words in the sentence rhyme, underline yes. If they do not, underline no. At first it was a little snow but then the wind began to blow. Do words in the sentence rhyme? Underline yes or no. At first it was a little snow but then the wind began to blow.

2. no

Assessment

Name _____ **Date** _____ **Score** _____

Grammar, Usage, and Mechanics

Directions for Teacher: Make a copy of page 129 from the Student Blackline Masters section for each student. Use the student's copy to record results.

Teacher: Listen carefully for this activity. You will answer different kinds of questions.

Teacher: You remember that exclamatory sentences show emotions. Listen to the sentence for Number 1. If it is an exclamatory sentence, draw a line under "yes." If it is not, draw a line under "no." *Quick, throw me the ball!* Is this an exclamatory sentence? Draw a line under "yes" or "no." *Quick, throw me the ball!*

1. yes   no

Teacher: Move down to Number 2. Listen carefully to this sentence. *A grasshopper can jump really far.* Is this an exclamatory sentence? Draw a line under "yes" or "no." *A grasshopper can jump really far.*

2. yes   no

Teacher: Look at the sentence for Number 3 as I read it out loud. *That is wonderful news!* Should this sentence end with an exclamation point? Draw a line under "yes" or "no." *That is wonderful news!*

3. That is wonderful news

yes   no

Teacher: Number 4 is a little different. You will show if an expanded sentence is correct. Listen to the first sentence. *Hurry up!* Now listen to the expanded sentence. *Hurry up, or we'll be late!* Is the expanded sentence correct? Draw a line under "yes" or "no." *Hurry up, or we'll be late!*

4. yes   no

Teacher: Move down to Number 5. Listen to the first sentence. *What is that?* Now listen to the expanded sentence. *What is beside so that?* Is the expanded sentence correct? Draw a line under "yes" or "no." *What is beside so that?*

5. yes   no

Phoneme Blending: Initial Sounds

Directions for Teacher: Duplicate page T130 for each student you choose to assess. Record results on this page.

Teacher: Put these word parts together and tell me the word. Are you ready? /b/ (pause for two seconds) *ake.*

1. ☐ bake

Teacher: Put these word parts together and tell me the word. Are you ready? /r/ (pause for two seconds) *ush.*

2. ☐ rush

Teacher: Put these word parts together and tell me the word. Are you ready? /g/ (pause for two seconds) *oat.*

3. ☐ goat

Teacher: Put these word parts together and tell me the word. Are you ready? /c/ (pause for two seconds) *old.*

4. ☐ cold

Teacher: Put these word parts together and tell me the word. Are you ready? /o/ (pause for two seconds) *ff.*

5. ☐ off

Assessment

Name _____ **Date** _____ **Score** _____

Letter Sounds

Directions for Teacher: Make a copy of page 131 from the Student Blackline Masters section for each student. Use the student's copy to record results.

Teacher: This activity is about letter sounds. Listen carefully to what I say. Draw a line under the letter you think is correct.

Teacher: The word in the box should be *got*. Which letter should go at the beginning of the word *got*? What sound does it make?

1.   h   g   s

Teacher: The word in the box should be *can*. Which letter should go at the beginning of the word *can*? What sound does it make?

2.    c   m   t

Teacher: The word in the box should be *red*. Which letter should go at the beginning of the word *red*? What sound does it make?

3. 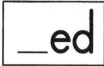   l   b   r

Teacher: The word in the box should be *leg*. Which letter should go at the end of the word *leg*? What sound does it make?

4. 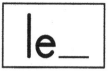   d   g   t

Teacher: The word in the box should be *rub*. Which letter should go at the end of the word *rub*? What sound does it make?

5.    b   n   g

Name _____ **Date** _____ **Score** ___

High-Frequency Words

Directions for Teacher: Make a copy of page 132 from the Student Blackline Masters section for each student. Use the student's copy to record results.

Teacher: This activity is about reading words. Look at these words. Read them to me one at a time, starting on the left.

can   his   on   him   did

Scoring:

☐ can ☐ his ☐ on ☐ him ☐ did   Total: ___

☐ Student read words at a pace that suggests they were recognized automatically.

Assessment

Name _____ **Date** _____ **Score** _____

Selection Vocabulary

Directions for Teacher: Make a copy of page 133 from the Student Blackline Masters section for each student. Use the student's copy to record results.

Teacher: Listen carefully to what I say. Draw a line under the answer you think is correct.

Teacher: Which picture shows a *bolt*? Draw a line under the picture that shows a *bolt*.

1.

Teacher: Which arrow points to a *support*? Draw a line under the picture in which the arrow points to a *support*.

2.

Teacher: Which picture shows something that is *clear*? Draw a line under the picture that shows something that is *clear*.

3.

Teacher: Which picture shows *diamonds*? Draw a line under the picture that shows *diamonds*.

4.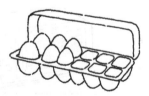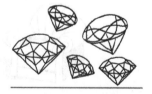

Teacher: Which picture shows a *knoll*? Draw a line under the picture that shows a *knoll*.

5.

Name _____ **Date** _____ **Score** _____

Sequence

Directions for Teacher: Make a copy of page 134 from the Student Blackline Masters section for each student. Use the student's copy to record results.

Teacher: Listen to each story I read. Pay attention to the order of things in the story. Look at the pictures for Number 1 and listen to this story. *A truck delivered the bricks. They were in a big pile on the ground. The workers made a wall with the bricks. Then they added a gate. The workers put trees in front of the wall beside the gate.* Draw a line under the picture that shows what it looked like just before the workers put the trees in.

1.

  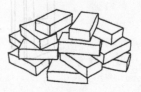

Teacher: Look at Number 2. Listen carefully. *The boy stood on the corner. It started to rain, so he ran under an awning. A friend came by, and she had an umbrella. They talked for a moment. Then the two of them walked to the store using the umbrella.* Draw a line under the picture showing what happened just after it started to rain.

2.

Text Features and Story Elements

Teacher: Look at the illustrations for Number 1 and listen to this question. *Which illustration would go best with a story about things in the kitchen?* Draw a line under the illustration that would go best with a story about kitchen things.

1.

Teacher: Move down to Number 2. This question is a little different. Listen to this story and look at the pictures. *When he left for school, Ming left his backpack on a chair. He didn't think about it on the bus. He only remembered the backpack when he got to his classroom. He was upset because he forgot his homework.* Draw a line under the picture that shows the problem that was introduced in the beginning of the story.

2.

Name _____ Date _____ Score _____

Grammar, Usage, and Mechanics

Directions for Teacher: Make a copy of page 135 from the Student Blackline Masters section for each student. Use the student's copy to record results.

Teacher: Look at the sentence for Number 1. Decide if the end punctuation is correct. *Be careful, the dish is hot!* Should this sentence end with an exclamation point? Draw a line under "yes" or "no."

1. Be careful, the dish is hot!

yes   no

Teacher: Move down to Number 2 and listen carefully. *Pears grow on trees.* Should this sentence end with an exclamation point? *Pears grow on trees.* Draw a line under "yes" or "no."

2. Pears grow on trees!

yes   no

Teacher: Look at the sentence for Number 3. *Surprise, here's your present!* Should this sentence end with a period? *Surprise, here's your present!* Draw a line under "yes" or "no."

3. Surprise, here's your present.

yes   no

Teacher: Move down to Number 4 and listen carefully. *Get out of the way of that car!* Should this sentence end with an exclamation point? *Get out of the way of that car!* Draw a line under "yes" or "no."

4. Get out of the way of that car!

yes   no

Teacher: Look at the sentence for Number 5. *Mars is a planet near Earth.* Should this sentence end with a period? *Mars is a planet near Earth.* Draw a line under "yes" or "no."

5. Mars is a planet near Earth.

yes   no

Assessment

Name _____ **Date** _____ **Score** _____

Letter Sounds

Directions for Teacher: Make a copy of page 136 from the Student Blackline Masters section for each student. Use the student's copy to record results.

Teacher: This activity is about the sounds letters make. Listen carefully to what I say. Draw a line under the answer you think is correct.

Hold up the letter c alphabet card.

Teacher: What letter is this? What sound does it make? Say the sound. Then underline the letter.

1.   <u>c</u>   r   g

Hold up the letter *b* alphabet card.
Teacher: What letter is this? What sound does it make? Say the sound. Then underline the letter.

2.   <u>b</u>   d   t

Hold up the letter *o* alphabet card.
Teacher: What letter is this? What sound does it make? Say the sound. Then underline the letter.

3.   a   i   <u>o</u>

Hold up the letter *r* alphabet card.
Teacher: What letter is this? What sound does it make? Say the sound. Then underline the letter.

4.   <u>r</u>   b   s

Hold up the letter *g* alphabet card.
Teacher: What letter is this? What sound does it make? Say the sound. Then underline the letter.

5.   h   <u>g</u>   s

Name _____ Date _____ Score _____

Phoneme Segmentation

Directions for Teacher: Duplicate page T137 for each student you choose to assess. Record results on this page.

Teacher: I will say a word. I want you to say the same word one sound at a time. Here's a practice word: *sat*. Say the word *sat* for me one sound at a time. /s/ /a/ /t/

Teacher: Say the word *leg* one sound at a time: *leg*.

1. ☐ /l/ /e/ /g/

Teacher: Say the word *pan* one sound at a time: *pan*.

2. ☐ /p/ /a/ /n/

Teacher: Say the word *not* one sound at a time: *not*.

3. ☐ /n/ /o/ /t/

Teacher: Say the word *stop* one sound at a time: *stop*.

4. ☐ /s/ /t/ /o/ /p/

Teacher: Say the word *mule* one sound at a time: *mule*.

5. ☐ /m/ /ū/ /l/

Alphabetic Principle

Directions for Teacher: Make a copy of pages 138–139 from the Student Blackline Masters section for each student. Use the student's copy to record results.

Teacher: This activity is about making new words. Listen carefully to what I say. Draw a line under the answer you think is correct.

Teacher: Which letter do you need to add to /b/ /a/ to make the word *bag*? What sound does the letter make?

1.   g̲   c   b

Teacher: Which letter do you need to add to /r/ /i/ to make the word *rib*? What sound does the letter make?

2.   p   b̲   d

Teacher: Which letter do you need to add to /h/ /a/ to make the word *hat*? What sound does the letter make?

3.   g   d   t̲

Teacher: Think about the word *lab*. If you take away the /l/, which letter can you add to /a/ /b/ to make the word *cab*? What sound does the letter make?

4.   t   c̲   g

Teacher: Think about the word *top*. If you take away the /t/, which letter can you add to /o/ /p/ to make the word *mop*? What sound does the letter make?

5.   p   m̲   n

Name _____ **Date** _____ **Score** _____

Alphabetic Principle

Teacher: Which letter do you need to add to /n/ /a/ to make the word *nap*? What sound does the letter make?

6. b   m   p̲

Teacher: Which letter do you need to add to /p/ /i/ to make the word *pit*? What sound does the letter make?

7. d   g   t̲

Teacher: Which letter do you need to add to /d/ /o/ to make the word *dog*? What sound does the letter make?

8. g̲   c   s

Teacher: Listen to the sounds I say: /l/ /i/ /p/. If you take away the /l/, which letter can you add to /i/ /p/ to make the word *sip*? What sound does the letter make?

9. r   c   s̲

Teacher: Listen to the sounds I say: /m/ /a/ /p/. If you take away the /m/, which letter can you add to /a/ /p/ to make the word *rap*? What sound does the letter make?

10. r̲   i   g

Name _____ Date _____ Score _____

Vocabulary

Directions for Teacher: Make a copy of page 140 from the Student Blackline Masters section for each student. Use the student's copy to record results.

Teacher: Listen carefully to what I say. Draw a line under the answer you think is correct.

Teacher: The word is *centuries. Centuries* are animals that live in trees. Draw a line under "yes" or "no." *Centuries* are animals that live in trees.

1.   yes   no

Teacher: The word is *fold.* You have to *fold* clothes sometimes to put them in a drawer. Draw a line under "yes" or "no." You have to *fold* clothes sometimes to put them in a drawer.

2.   yes   no

Teacher: The word is *recycle.* To *recycle* means to ride in a plane. Draw a line under "yes" or "no." To *recycle* means to ride in a plane.

3.   yes   no

Teacher: The word is *save.* It is a good idea to *save* money so you can buy things that are important. Draw a line under "yes" or "no." It is a good idea to *save* money so you can buy things that are important.

4.   yes   no

Teacher: The word is *holiday.* The day before yesterday is called *holiday.* Draw a line under "yes" or "no." The day before yesterday is called *holiday.*

5.   yes   no

Teacher: The word is *wink.* To *wink* is to drive very fast. Draw a line under "yes" or "no." To *wink* is to drive very fast.

6.   yes   no

Name _____ **Date** _____ **Score** _____

Comprehension

Directions for Teacher: Make a copy of pages 141–142 from the Student Blackline Masters section for each student. Use the student's copy to record results.

Teacher: Look at the pictures for Number 1. Draw a line under the two pictures that go together because they show things that keep you dry in the rain...keep you dry in the rain.

1.

Teacher: Look at the pictures for Number 2. Draw a line under the two pictures that go together because they show kinds of weather...kinds of weather.

2.

Teacher: Look at the pictures for Number 3. Listen to this story. *A spider's web is very strong. It is also sticky. When bugs fly into the web, they get stuck. The web helps the spider catch food.* Draw a line under the picture that shows what this story is mostly about.

3.

  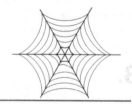

Teacher: Move down to Number 4. Listen to this story. *A pyramid is a kind of stone building. It is in the shape of a triangle. People long ago made pyramids in different places.* Draw a line under the picture that shows what shape a pyramid has.

4.

 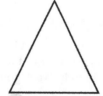 

Teacher: Look at the pictures for Number 5. *Saturday was a busy day for Elena. She had breakfast and then went for a run. She got cleaned up and visited her grandfather. After that, she went food shopping with her mother. In the afternoon, she read her book.* Draw a line under the picture that shows what Elena did after visiting her grandfather.

5.

Name _____ **Date** _____ **Score** _____

Comprehension

Teacher: Listen carefully to what I say. You will be doing different things in this activity.

Teacher: Look at the picture for Number 6. Listen to this caption. Does it tell about the picture? *The space station is high above Earth.* Draw a line under "yes" or "no." Do the words match the picture? *The space station is high above Earth.*

6.    yes   <u>no</u>

Teacher: Now we will do something different. Move down to Number 7. Look at the illustrations and listen to this question. *Which illustration would go best with a story about animals with stripes?* Draw a line under the illustration that would go best with a story about animals with stripes?

7.

Teacher: Look at the pictures for Number 8. Listen to this story. *The tree fell down in the storm. It blocked the road so traffic backed up. Some people drove on the bridge instead of the road.* Draw a line under the picture that shows the problem that was introduced in the beginning of the story.

8.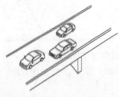

Teacher: In this part of the activity, we will do something different. Listen carefully to the directions.

Teacher: Look at the answers for Number 9. You learned about exclamatory sentences before. These sentences express strong emotions or feelings. Listen to this sentence. It is an exclamatory sentence. *Wow, you hit a home run!* Underline the correct end mark. *Wow, you hit a home run!*

9.   ?   <u>!</u>

Teacher: Number 10 is a little different. Listen carefully. You learned about imperative sentences before. These sentences give a command. Listen to this sentence. It is an imperative sentence and gives a command, *Tell George to stop shouting.* Underline the correct end mark. *Tell George to stop shouting.*

10.   ?   !

Name _____ Date _____ Score _____

Grammar, Usage, and Mechanics

Directions for Teacher: Make a copy of page 143 from the Student Blackline Masters section for each student. Use the student's copy to record results.

Teacher: Listen carefully to what I say. You will be doing different things in this activity.

Teacher: Look at the answers for Number 1. You learned about exclamatory sentences before. These sentences express strong emotions or feelings. Listen to this sentence. If it is an exclamatory sentence, underline "yes." If it is not an exclamatory sentence, underline "no." *Did you see my book?* Is this an exclamatory sentence? Underline "yes" or "no." *Did you see my book?*

1. yes   <u>no</u>

Teacher: Move down to Number 2. Listen to this sentence. *Ouch, that thorn stuck me!* If it is an exclamatory sentence, underline "yes." If it is not an exclamatory sentence, underline "no." *Ouch, that thorn stuck me!*

2. <u>yes</u>   no

Teacher: Look at the sentence for Number 3 as I read it out loud. Decide if the end punctuation is correct. *Here is your lunch.* Should this sentence end with an exclamation point? Draw a line under "yes" or "no." *Here is your lunch.*

3. Here is your lunch!

yes   <u>no</u>

Teacher: Number 4 is a little different. You will show if an expanded sentence is correct. Listen to the first sentence. *Run quickly!* Now listen to the expanded sentence. *Run quickly, a storm is coming!* Is the expanded sentence correct? Mark "yes" or "no." *Run quickly, a storm is coming!*

4. <u>yes</u>   no

Teacher: Move down to Number 5. Listen to this sentence and look at the punctuation marks. *How long is this movie?* Draw a line under the punctuation mark that should come at the end of the sentence. *How long is this movie?*

5. .   !   <u>?</u>

Name _____ **Date** _____ **Score** ____

Letter Sounds

Directions for Teacher: Duplicate page T144 for each student you choose to assess. Record results on this page.

Teacher: When you spell *jar*, what letter comes first? What sound does it make?

1. ☐ j   ☐ /j/

Teacher: When you spell *fix*, what letter comes first? What sound does it make?

2. ☐ f   ☐ /f/

Teacher: When you spell *leaf*, what letter comes last? What sound does it make?

3. ☐ f   ☐ /f/

Teacher: When you spell *just*, what letter comes first? What sound does it make?

4. ☐ j   ☐ /j/

Teacher: When you spell *roof*, what letter comes last? What sound does it make?

5. ☐ f   ☐ /f/

Name _____ **Date** _____ **Score** ____

Phoneme Manipulation: Initial and Final Sounds

Directions for Teacher: Duplicate page T145 for each student you choose to assess. Record results on this page.

Teacher: Listen to this word: *ring*. If you change the first sound to /s/, what new word do you have? The word is *ring*; change the first sound to /s/.

1. ☐ sing

Teacher: Listen to this word: *fair*. If you change the first sound to /h/, what new word do you have? The word is *fair*; change the first sound to /h/.

2. ☐ hair

Teacher: Listen to this word: *may*. If you change the first sound to /s/, what new word do you have? The word is *may*; change the first sound to /s/.

3. ☐ say

Teacher: Listen to this word: *ant*. If you change the last sound to /d/, what new word do you have? The word is *ant*; change the last sound to /d/.

4. ☐ and

Teacher: Listen to this word: *pig*. If you change the last sound to /n/, what new word do you have? The word is *pig*; change the last sound to /n/.

5. ☐ pin

Name _____ **Date** _____ **Score** _____

Selection Vocabulary

Directions for Teacher: Make a copy of page 146 from the Student Blackline Masters section for each student. Use the student's copy to record results.

Teacher: Listen carefully to what I say. Draw a line under the answer you think is correct.

Teacher: Which picture shows something with *cracks*? Draw a line under the picture that shows something with *cracks*.

1.

Teacher: Which picture shows *decorations*? Draw a line under the picture that shows *decorations*.

2.

Teacher: Which picture shows a box that is *filled*? Draw a line under the picture that shows a box that is *filled*.

3.

Teacher: Which picture shows how to *hold* a ball? Draw a line under the picture that shows how to *hold* a ball.

4.

Teacher: If someone *seals* a box, is it closed or open? Draw a line under your answer. If someone *seals* a box, is it closed or open?

5.

Assessment

Name _____ Date _____ Score _____

Classify and Categorize

Directions for Teacher: Make a copy of page 147 from the Student Blackline Masters section for each student. Use the student's copy to record results.

Teacher: In this activity, you will think about things that are alike.

Teacher: Look at the pictures for Number 1. Draw a line under the two pictures that go together because they show things that are electric tools...things that are electric tools.

1.

Teacher: Move down to Number 2. Look at the pictures. Draw a line under the picture that is most like a soccer ball because it is filled with air...like a soccer ball because it is filled with air.

2.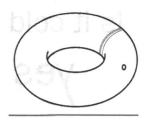

Story Elements

Directions for Teacher: This activity is about the setting and characters in stories. These are the places a story happens and the people or animals in the story.

Teacher: Listen carefully and look at the pictures for Number 1. *The wagon train moved slowly across the desert. Not much grew there except a cactus and a few trees. It was hot and dry, but it looked like a storm was coming in.* Draw a line under the picture that shows where this story takes place.

1.

Teacher: Look at the pictures for Number 2. *When the farmer went to the barn, the cows were not there. The wind had blown the door open. The farmer got on the horse and started looking for the cows. He heard his dog barking and went toward her. The dog found the cows in a neighbor's field.* Draw a line under the picture that shows who found the cows.

2.

Name _____ **Date** _____ **Score** _____

Grammar, Usage, and Mechanics

Directions for Teacher: Make a copy of page 148 from the Student Blackline Masters section for each student. Use the student's copy to record results.

Teacher: This activity is about sentences. Listen carefully to what I say and look at the sentences.

Teacher: Look at the sentence for Number 1. Is there a space between the sentences? Draw a line under "yes" or "no."

1. The sun was setting.I watched the sunset.

yes   <u>no</u>

Teacher: Move down to Number 2 and look at the sentences. Is there a space between the sentences? Draw a line under "yes" or "no."

2. Is it cold outside? You might need a coat.

<u>yes</u>   no

Teacher: Look at Number 3. Look at the sentences. Is there a space between the sentences? Draw a line under "yes" or "no." The moon shined. We gazed at it.

3. The moon shined. We gazed at it.

<u>yes</u>   no

Teacher: Move down to Number 4. Look at the sentences. Is there a space between the sentences? Draw a line under "yes" or "no." Bowling is fun!We go every week.

4. Bowling is fun!We go every week.

yes   <u>no</u>

Teacher: Move down to Number 5. Look at the sentences. Is there a space between the sentences? Draw a line under "yes" or "no." The bus is late.Will it be here soon?

5. The bus is late.Will it be here soon?

yes   <u>no</u>

Name _____ **Date** _____ **Score** _____

Letter Sounds

Directions for Teacher: Duplicate page T149 for each student you choose to assess. Record results on this page.

Teacher: When you say *up*, what letter makes the first sound? What sound does it make?

1. ☐ u ☐ /ə/

Teacher: When you spell *fox*, what letter comes last? What sound does it make?

2. ☐ x ☐ /ks/

Teacher: When you spell *sun*, what letter comes in the middle? What sound does it make?

3. ☐ u ☐ /ə/

Teacher: When you say *box*, what letter makes the last sound? What sound does it make?

4. ☐ x ☐ /ks/

Teacher: When you spell *but*, what letter comes in the middle? What sound does it make?

5. ☐ u ☐ /ə/

Assessment

Name _____ **Date** _____ **Score** _____

Phoneme Blending: Initial Sounds

Directions for Teacher: Duplicate page T150 for each student you choose to assess. Record results on this page.

Teacher: Put these word parts together and tell me the word. Are you ready? *foo* (pause for two seconds) /t/

1. ☐ foot

Teacher: Put these word parts together and tell me the word. Are you ready? *dee* (pause for two seconds) /p/

2. ☐ deep

Teacher: Put these word parts together and tell me the word. Are you ready? *car* (pause for two seconds) /d/

3. ☐ card

Teacher: Put these word parts together and tell me the word. Are you ready? *thin* (pause for two seconds) /k/

4. ☐ think

Teacher: Put these word parts together and tell me the word. Are you ready? *pi* (pause for two seconds) /n/

5. ☐ pin

Assessment

Name _____ **Date** _____ **Score** _____

Selection Vocabulary

Directions for Teacher: Make a copy of page 151 from the Student Blackline Masters section for each student. Use the student's copy to record results.

Teacher: Listen carefully to what I say. Draw a line under the answer you think is correct.

Teacher: Which picture shows what you use to *scrub* things? Draw a line under the picture that shows what you use to *scrub* things.

1.

 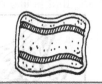

Teacher: Which picture shows a *band*? Draw a line under the picture that shows a *band*.

2.

Teacher: Which picture shows a *magazine*? Draw a line under the picture that shows a *magazine*.

3.

Teacher: Which picture shows a *reason* why someone might get wet? Draw a line under the picture that shows a *reason* why someone might get wet.

4.

Teacher: Which picture shows a *cactus*? Draw a line under the picture that shows a *cactus*.

5.

Name _____ Date _____ Score _____

Compare and Contrast

Directions for Teacher: Make a copy of page 152 from the Student Blackline Masters section for each student. Use the student's copy to record results.

Teacher: In this activity, you will think about how things are alike or different. Listen carefully to what I say. Look at the pictures and think about the question.

Teacher: Look at the pictures for Number 1. The picture in the box is a frog. Draw a line under the other picture of something that is like the frog because it lives in water.

1.

Teacher: Look at the pictures for Number 2. The picture in the box is a cane Draw a line under the other picture of something that is different from a cane because it does *not* help you walk.

2.

Text Features

Directions for Teacher: This activity is about dialogue and punctuation. Students learned before that dialogue means characters in a story are talking.

Teacher: Look at the answers for Number 1. Listen to the sentence. Think about what kind of punctuation mark it needs. *Do you want a smoothie for breakfast?* Draw a line under the correct end mark. *Do you want a smoothie for breakfast?*

1. . ? !

Teacher: Move down to Number 2. Look at the sentences. Draw a line under the quotation marks...just the quotation marks.

2. "This is wonderful soup," said Raj.
His father smiled at him.

Assessment

Name _____ Date _____ Score _____

Grammar, Usage, and Mechanics

Directions for Teacher: Make a copy of page 153 from the Student Blackline Masters section for each student. Use the student's copy to record results.

Teacher: In this activity, you will answer different kinds of questions. Be sure to listen carefully so you know what you are supposed to do.

Teacher: For Number 1, you must decide if a sentence has repeated sounds. Listen to what I say. If you hear repeated sounds, underline "yes." If not, underline "no." *The bashful bear began to sing.* Are sounds repeated in the sentence? Underline "yes" or "no." *The bashful bear began to sing.*

1. <u>yes</u>   no

Teacher: Move down to Number 2 and listen for repeated sounds. *The seagull flew over the beach.* Are sounds repeated in the sentence? Underline "yes" or "no." *The seagull flew over the beach.*

2. yes   <u>no</u>

Teacher: Look at the pictures for Number 3. The pictures show a sitting rabbit, a running rabbit, and an eating rabbit. Which picture shows repeated sounds? Draw a line under your answer.

3.

Teacher: Move down to Number 4 and look at the pictures. They show a round compass, pretty flower, and towering tree. Which picture shows repeated sounds? Draw a line under your answer.

4.

Teacher: Move down to Number 5 and look at the pictures. They show a curious cat, a friendly dog, and a singing bird. Which picture shows repeated sounds? Draw a line under your answer.

5.

Assessment   **T153**

Name _____ **Date** _____ **Score** _____

Letter Sounds

Directions for Teacher: Make a copy of page 154 from the Student Blackline Masters section for each student. Use the student's copy to record results.

Teacher: This activity is about letter sounds. Listen carefully to what I say. Draw a line under the letter you think is correct.

Teacher: Which letter should go at the beginning of the word *jet*? What sound does it make?

1.   j̲   g   r

Teacher: Which letter should go at the beginning of the word *fit*? What sound does it make?

2.   h   m   f̲

Teacher: Which letter should go at the beginning of the word *up*? What sound does it make?

3.   m   u̲   c

Teacher: Which letter should go at the end of the word *fix*? What sound does it make?

4.   x̲   n   c

Teacher: Which letter should go at the end of the word *whiz*? What sound does it make?

5. 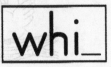   m   z̲   t

Assessment

Name _____ Date _____ Score _____

High-Frequency Words

Directions for Teacher: Make a copy of page 155 from the Student Blackline Masters section for each student. Use the student's copy to record results.

Teacher: This activity is about words you have learned. Listen carefully to what I say. Draw a line under the word you think is correct.

Teacher: The word is *for. I play for my school.* Draw a line under *for.*

1.   of   all   <u>for</u>

Teacher: The word is *but. Jeff called, but Steve was not home.* Draw a line under *but.*

2.   <u>but</u>   am   go

Teacher: The word is *up. The path goes up the hill.* Draw a line under *up.*

3.   do   <u>up</u>   of

Teacher: The word is *all. I finished all the chores.* Draw a line under *all.*

4.   <u>all</u>   at   am

Teacher: The word is *girl. The girl liked to paint.* Draw a line under *girl.*

5.   his   <u>girl</u>   had

Name _____ Date _____ Score _____

Selection Vocabulary

Directions for Teacher: Make a copy of page 156 from the Student Blackline Masters section for each student. Use the student's copy to record results.

Teacher: Listen carefully to what I say. Draw a line under the answer you think is correct.

Teacher: Which picture shows a *bay*? Draw a line under the picture that shows a *bay*.

1.

Teacher: Which picture shows someone who will *collect* fruit? Draw a line under the picture that shows someone who will *collect* fruit.

2.

Teacher: Which picture shows a *mirror*? Draw a line under the picture that shows a *mirror*.

3.

Teacher: Which picture shows a *plain* shirt? Draw a line under the picture that shows a *plain* shirt.

4.

Teacher: Which picture shows how to *strain* something? Draw a line under the picture that shows how to *strain* something.

5.

Assessment

Name _____ **Date** _____ **Score** _____

Cause and Effect

Directions for Teacher: Make a copy of page 157 from the Student Blackline Masters section for each student. Use the student's copy to record results.

Teacher: You learned before about causes and effects. This activity will give you a chance to practice what you learned.

Teacher: Listen to the story for Number 1. *A little path went up the hill. June wondered what made it. The path was too small for people. She thought it was too big for rabbits. Her mother said coyotes made the path by walking up and down the hill.* Draw a line under the picture that shows the cause of the path.

1.

Teacher: Listen to the story for Number 2. This one is a little different. *Tim put a pen in his shirt pocket. It leaked and stained his shirt. He put a coat on and hoped no one would see the stain.* Draw a line under the picture that shows the effect of the leaky pen.

2.

Genre Knowledge

Teacher: You will do different things in this activity. Be sure to listen carefully so you will know what to do.

Teacher: This question is about realistic fiction, or stories that seem like real life. Listen to the story and decide if it is realistic fiction. *Vik handed his mom the permission slip. She needed to sign it for him. Then he could go to the zoo next week!* Is this realistic fiction? Draw a line under "yes" or "no."

1.   no

Teacher: Move down to Number 2. Listen to the story and decide if it is realistic fiction. *The giant blew his horn. His pet dragon flew to him. The dragon breathed fire to cook the giant's food.* Is this realistic fiction? Draw a line under "yes" or "no."

2.   no

Name _____ **Date** _____ **Score** _____

Grammar, Usage, and Mechanics

Directions for Teacher: Make a copy of page 158 from the Student Blackline Masters section for each student. Use the student's copy to record results.

Teacher: You will be doing different things in this activity, so be sure to listen carefully.

Teacher: Look at the sentence for Number 1. Count the number of spaces between the words in the sentence. Draw a line under the number that shows how many spaces there are in the sentence.

1. The game started at noon.

2   3   <u>4</u>

Teacher: Move down to Number 2. Listen carefully. Count the number of spaces between the sentences. Draw a line under the number that shows how many spaces there are between the sentences.

2. Bob saw Dot. He waved to her. She came over. They talked for a bit.

2   <u>3</u>   4

Teacher: Look at Number 3. If the sentence starts with a capital letter and ends with a period, draw a line under "yes." If it does not, draw a line under "no." Does the sentence start with a capital letter and end with a period?

3. Our flag has stars and stripes.

<u>yes</u>   no

Teacher: Move down to Number 4. Listen carefully. I will read two sentences. You will tell me if the second one is correct. Listen carefully to the first sentence. *The park is pretty.* Now listen to the expanded sentence. *The park that is a park is pretty.* Is the expanded sentence correct? Mark "yes" or "no." *The park that is a park is pretty.*

4.   yes   <u>no</u>

Teacher: Look at the answers for Number 5. Listen to this sentence. The soup was hot. Now I will read a sentence with describing words. *The soup was so hot that Carol couldn't eat it.* Is the expanded sentence a good way to describe how hot the soup was? Draw a line under "yes" or "no." *The soup was so hot that Carol couldn't eat it.*

5.   <u>yes</u>   no

Name _____ **Date** _____ **Score** _____

Phonemic Awareness: Phoneme Segmentation

Directions for the Teacher

This assessment is intended to be administered to students individually. Duplicate page T160 for each student. You will record the student's responses on the page.

Sit at a table that allows you and the student to work comfortably. You may find it easier to sit across from the student rather than beside the student.

For the words *band* through *has*, tell children: **I will say a word. You will say the first sound of that word. Then you will say the whole word. Here is a practice word:** sat. /s/ sat.

You may repeat the practice activity several more times until you are sure the student knows what to do. Some other words you may use are *lift*, *tug*, and *hip*. Check the box beside each word the student segments correctly.

For the words *fill* through *hold*, tell children: **This one is a little different. I will say a word. You will say the last sound of that word. Then you will say the whole word: Here is a practice word:** cup. /p/ cup.

After you have completed the assessment, record the number correct on the page and on the STUDENT ASSESSMENT RECORD and CLASS ASSESSMENT RECORD. If any students do not meet the recommended performance level, repeat the assessment after intervention or additional instruction.

Name _____ **Date** _____ **Score** _____

Phonemic Awareness:
Phoneme Segmentation

☐ band /b/ /a/ /n/ /d/

☐ nut /n/ /u/ /t/

☐ man /m/ /a/ /n/

☐ rob /r/ /o/ /b/

☐ has /h/ /a/ /s/

☐ fill /f/ /i/ /l/

☐ jut /j/ /u/ /t/

☐ gift /g/ /i/ /f/ /t/

☐ ax /a/ /ks/

☐ hold /h/ /ō/ /l/ /d/

Phoneme Segmentation total: _____

Name _____ **Date** _____ **Score** _____

Phoneme Blending: Final Sounds

Directions for Teacher: Duplicate page T161 for each student you choose to assess. Record results on this page.

Teacher: Put these word parts together and tell me the word. Are you ready? *pu* (pause for two seconds) /f/

1. ☐ puff

Teacher: Put these word parts together and tell me the word. Are you ready? *fi* (pause for two seconds) /z/

2. ☐ fizz

Teacher: Put these word parts together and tell me the word. Are you ready? *bu* (pause for two seconds) /z/

3. ☐ buzz

Teacher: Put these word parts together and tell me the word. Are you ready? *si* (pause for two seconds) /ks/

4. ☐ six

Teacher: Put these word parts together and tell me the word. Are you ready? *spot* (pause for two seconds) /z/

5. ☐ spots

Name _____ **Date** _____ **Score** _____

Letter Sounds

Directions for Teacher: Duplicate page T162 for each student you choose to assess. Record results on this page.

Teacher: When you say *jet*, what letter makes the first sound? What is the first sound?

1. ☐ j   ☐ /j/

Teacher: When you say *knife*, what sound comes last?

2. ☐ /f/

Teacher: When you spell *six*, what letter comes last? What is the last sound?

3. ☐ x   ☐ /ks/

Teacher: When you say *zoo*, what letter makes the first sound? What is the first sound?

4. ☐ z   ☐ /z/

Teacher: When you spell *mud*, what letter comes in the middle? What is the middle sound?

5. ☐ u   ☐ /u/

Name _____ Date _____ Score _____

Print Concepts

Directions for Teacher

This assessment is intended to be administered individually using a decodable book with which the student is familiar.

Duplicate page T163 for each student you choose to assess. You will record the student's responses on this page. After you have completed the assessment, write the number correct in the space at the bottom of the page and on the STUDENT ASSESSMENT RECORD and CLASS ASSESSMENT RECORD.

Sit at a table that allows you and the student to work comfortably. Put the book on the table with the cover down. Ask the following questions and check each question the student answers correctly.

☐ Show me the front cover of this book.

☐ Show me the back cover of this book.

(For the following three items, be sure the cover of the book or the title page is showing.)

☐ Point to the title of the book.

☐ Show me the name of the person who wrote the book, the author.

☐ Now show me the name of the person who drew the pictures in the book, the illustrator.

(For the following questions, be sure the student opens the book to a typical two-page spread with an illustration.)

☐ Open the book. Show me a page number.

☐ Point to a word on the page.

☐ Point to an illustration on the page. An illustration is a picture.

☐ Point to a space between words. How about another space between words?

☐ Run your finger under a sentence. Show me where the sentence begins and ends.

☐ If you were reading this page, show me the word you would read first.

☐ Now show me the words you would read next. Move your fingers to show me the direction you would read the words.

☐ After you finish reading the first line on this page, point to the line you would read next and where you would start reading.

☐ After you finish reading this page, show me what page you would read next.

Print Concepts total: _____

Name _____ Date _____ Score _____

Vocabulary

Directions for Teacher: Make a copy of page 164 from the Student Blackline Masters section for each student. Use the student's copy to record results.

Teacher: Listen carefully to what I say. Draw a line under the answer you think is correct.

Teacher: The word is *other*. This door is locked, so we will have to use the *other* one. Draw a line under "yes" or "no." This door is locked, so we will have to use the *other* one.

1. yes   no

Teacher: The word is *tradition*. A *tradition* is a chair that holds more than one person. Draw a line under "yes" or "no." A *tradition* is a chair that holds more than one person.

2. yes   no

Teacher: The word is *culture*. We learned about the *culture* of people from long ago who made things of wood and clay. Draw a line under "yes" or "no." We learned about the *culture* of people from long ago who made things of wood and clay.

3. yes   no

Teacher: The word is *talents*. *Talents* are snacks made out of cereal. Draw a line under "yes" or "no." *Talents* are snacks made out of cereal.

4. yes   no

Teacher: The word is *influence*. *Influence* means about the same as paint. Draw a line under "yes" or "no." *Influence* means about the same as paint.

5. yes   no

Teacher: The word is *wrap*. When you *wrap* something, you cut it in half. Draw a line under "yes" or "no." When you *wrap* something, you cut it in half.

6. yes   no

Name _____ **Date** _____ **Score** _____

Comprehension

Directions for Teacher: Make a copy of pages 165–166 from the Student Blackline Masters section for each student. Use the student's copy to record results.

Teacher: In this activity, you will answer different kinds of questions. Listen carefully so you will know what to do. Think about what I said before choosing an answer.

Teacher: Look at the pictures for Number 1. This is a little different. Look at the pictures. Draw a line under the two pictures that go together because they show things that protect your head...things that protect your head.

1.

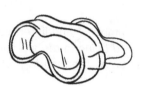

Teacher: Move down to Number 2. Draw a line under the two pictures that go together because they show people together as a team...people playing sports as a team.

2.

Teacher: Look at the pictures for Number 3. The picture in the box shows toy blocks. Draw a line under the other picture of something that is like the blocks because you play with it.

3.

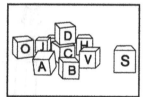  

Teacher: Look at the pictures for Number 4. The picture in the box is an airplane. Draw a line under the other picture of something that is different from an airplane because it does *not* fly.

4.

  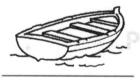

Teacher: Move down to Number 5. Listen carefully. *Vanna went for a hike with her friends. They wore backpacks and brought hiking poles. They wore bells on their boots to keep bears away. They had a wonderful time.* Draw a line under the thing that kept the bears away.

5.

Name _____ **Date** _____ **Score** _____

Comprehension

Teacher: Listen carefully to what I say because you will be doing different things in this activity.

Teacher: Look at the answers for Number 6. This question is about realistic fiction, stories that seem like real life. Listen to the story and decide if it is realistic fiction. *Some people waited outside the store. It wasn't open yet because it was early in the morning.* Is this story like real life? Draw a line under "yes" or "no."

6. <u>yes</u>   no

Teacher: Now we will do something a little different. Look at the pictures for Number 7 and listen carefully. *Randy was really excited. He was at his first professional baseball game. He loved being in the stadium with thousands of other people. The game would start in a few minutes.* Draw a line under the picture that shows where this story takes place.

7.

Teacher: Listen carefully and look at the pictures for Number 8. You will answer a question about the characters in the story. *Ed put some seeds in the bird feeder. His sister Anita took pictures of the birds when they came to the feeder. Their father waited for them in the kitchen.* Draw a line under the character who was taking pictures of the birds.

8.

Teacher: Look at the answers for Number 9. Listen to this sentence. Decide what punctuation mark it should end with. *Kyra bought a jug of milk at the corner store.* What punctuation mark should the sentence end with? Draw a line under your answer. *Kyra bought a jug of milk at the corner store.*

9.  .   ?   !

Teacher: Move down to Number 10. Listen to this sentence and decide what punctuation mark it should end with. *How long is an alligator?* What punctuation mark should the sentence end with? Draw a line under your answer. *How long is an alligator?*

10.   .   ?   !

Assessment

Name _____ **Date** _____ **Score** _____

Grammar, Usage, and Mechanics

Directions for Teacher: Make a copy of page 167 from the Student Blackline Masters section for each student. Use the student's copy to record results.

Teacher: You will be doing different things in this activity, so be sure to listen carefully.

Teacher: Look at the sentence for Number 1. Count the number of spaces between the words in the sentence. Draw a line under the number that shows how many spaces there are in the sentence.

1. Small fish swam in the pond.

3   4   <u>5</u>

Teacher: Move down to Number 2. Listen carefully. Count the number of spaces between the sentences. Draw a line under the number that shows how many spaces there are between the sentences.

2. Bart threw the ball to Laura. She caught it and threw it back to him.

<u>1</u>   2   3

Teacher: Look at Number 3. If the sentence starts with a capital letter and ends with a punctuation mark, draw a line under "yes." If it does not, draw a line under "no." Does the sentence start with a capital letter and end with a punctuation mark?

3. can I borrow your pen?

yes   <u>no</u>

Teacher: Move down to Number 4. Listen carefully. I will read two sentences. You will tell me if the second one is correct. Listen carefully to the first sentence. *The dog is Julie's.* Now listen to the expanded sentence. *The big brown dog is Julie's.* Is the expanded sentence correct? Mark "yes" or "no." *The big brown dog is Julie's.*

4. <u>yes</u>   no

Teacher: Look at the answers for Number 5. Listen to this sentence. *Chester is my dog.* Now I will read a sentence with describing words. *Chester is my big, brown dog.* Is the expanded sentence a good way to describe the dog? Draw a line under "yes" or "no." *Chester is my big, brown dog.*

5. <u>yes</u>   no

Lesson and Unit Assessment

Unit 1 Class Assessment Record

Student Name	Letter Recognition p. 15	Selection Vocabulary p. 16	Main Idea and Details Story Element: Plot p. 17	Grammar, Usage, and Mechanics p. 18	Phonemic Awareness: Word Sequence p. 20	Letter Recognition p. 21	Phonemic Awareness: Word Sequence p. 23	Selection Vocabulary p. 24	Classify and Categorize Genre Knowledge and Language Use p. 25

Lesson and Unit Assessment

Unit 1 Class Assessment Record

Student Name	Grammar, Usage, and Mechanics p. 26	Letter Recognition p. 27	Letter Recognition p. 28	Phonemic Awareness: Rhyme Production p. 30	Letter Recognition p. 32	Letter Recognition p. 33	Letter Recognition p. 34	Letter Recognition p. 35	Selection Vocabulary p. 36

Assessment

Lesson and Unit Assessment

Unit 1 Class Assessment Record

Student Name	Compare and Contrast, Story Elements p. 37	Grammar, Usage, and Mechanics p. 38	Unit 1 Assessment: Listening for Sounds p. 39	Unit 1 Assessment: Listening for Words p. 40	Unit 1 Assessment: Rhyming Words p. 41	Unit 1 Assessment: Selection Vocabulary p. 42	Unit 1 Assessment: Comprehension pp. 43–44	Unit 1 Assessment: Grammar, Usage, and Mechanics p. 45

Assessment

Lesson and Unit Assessment

Unit 2 Class Assessment Record

Student Name	Counting Words in Sentences p. 46	Identifying Spoken Sentences p. 47	Alphabet Sequence p. 49	Selection Vocabulary p. 50	Sequence, Genre Knowledge p. 51	Grammar, Usage, and Mechanics p. 52	Substituting Words in Rhymes p. 53	Alphabet Sequence p. 55	Word Part Blending p. 56

Lesson and Unit Assessment

Unit 2 Class Assessment Record

Student Name	Selection Vocabulary p. 57	Cause and Effect, Text Features p. 58	Grammar, Usage, and Mechanics p. 59	Syllable Blending and Segmentation p. 60	Selection Vocabulary p. 61	Main Idea and Details, Story Elements p. 62	Grammar, Usage, and Mechanics p. 63	Unit 2 Assessment: Word Part Blending p. 64

Unit 2 Class Assessment Record

Student Name	Unit 2 Assessment: Syllable Blending and Segmentation p. 65	Unit 2 Assessment: High-Frequency Words pp. 66–67	Unit 2 Assessment: Print Concepts p. 68	Unit 2 Assessment: Selection Vocabulary p. 69	Unit 2 Assessment: Comprehension p. 70–71	Unit 2 Assessment: Grammar, Usage, and Mechanics p. 72

Lesson and Unit Assessment

Unit 3 Class Assessment Record

Student Name	Blending Word Parts p. 73	Phoneme Matching: Initial Sounds p. 74	Selection Vocabulary p. 75	Classify and Categorize, Text Features p. 76	Grammar, Usage, and Mechanics p. 77	Phoneme Blending: Final Sounds p. 78	Letter Sounds p. 79	Selection Vocabulary p. 80

Lesson and Unit Assessment

Unit 3 Class Assessment Record

Student Name	Compare and Contrast p. 81	Grammar, Usage, and Mechanics p. 82	Letter Sounds p. 83	Blending Initial Sounds p. 84	High-Frequency Words p. 85	Selection Vocabulary p. 86	Cause and Effect, Story Elements p. 87

Assessment

Lesson and Unit Assessment

Unit 3 Class Assessment Record

Student Name	Grammar, Usage, and Mechanics p. 88	Unit 3 Assessment: Letters and Sounds p. 89	Unit 3 Assessment: Beginning Sounds p. 90	Unit 3 Assessment: Print Concepts p. 91	Unit 3 Assessment: Selection Vocabulary p. 92	Unit 3 Assessment: Comprehension, Text Features, Story Elements p. 93-94	Unit 3 Assessment: Grammar, Usage, and Mechanics p. 95

Unit 4 Class Assessment Record

Student Name	Blending Initial Sounds p. 96	Blending Final Sounds p. 97	Selection Vocabulary p. 98	Main Idea and Details, Genre Knowledge p. 99	Grammar, Usage, and Mechanics p. 100	Letter Sounds p. 101	Phoneme Manipulation: Initial Sounds p. 102

Lesson and Unit Assessment

Unit 4 Class Assessment Record

Student Name	Selection Vocabulary p. 103	Sequence, Text Features P. 104	Grammar, Usage, and Mechanics p. 105	Short-Vowel Sounds p. 106	High-Frequency Words p. 107-108	Segmenting: Onset and Rime p. 109	Selection Vocabulary p. 110	Cause and Effect, Story Elements p. 111

Lesson and Unit Assessment

Unit 4 Class Assessment Record

Student Name	Grammar, Usage, and Mechanics p. 112	Unit 4 Assessment: Letters and Sounds p. 113	Unit 4 Assessment: Ending Sounds p. 114	Unit 4 Assessment: Segmenting: Onset and Rime p. 115	Unit 4 Assessment: Selection Vocabulary p. 116	Unit 4 Assessment: Comprehension pp. 117-118	Unit 4 Assessment: Grammar, Usage, and Mechanics p. 119

Lesson and Unit Assessment

Unit 5 Class Assessment Record

Student Name	Letter Sounds p. 120	Phoneme Segmentation p. 121	Selection Vocabulary p. 122	Classify and Categorize, Text Features, Language Use p. 123	Grammar, Usage, and Mechanics p. 124	Letter Sounds p. 125	Phoneme Matching: Initial and Final Sounds p. 126	Selection Vocabulary p. 127

Assessment

Lesson and Unit Assessment

Unit 5 Class Assessment Record

Student Name	Main Idea and Details, Language Use p. 128	Grammar, Usage, and Mechanics p. 129	Phoneme Blending: Initial Sounds p. 130	Letter Sounds p. 131	High-Frequency Words p. 132	Selection Vocabulary p. 133	Sequence, Text Features, Story Elements p. 134

Assessment

Lesson and Unit Assessment

Unit 5 Class Assessment Record

Student Name	Grammar, Usage, and Mechanics p. 135	Unit 5 Assessment: Letter Sounds p. 136	Unit 5 Assessment: Phoneme Segmentation p. 137	Unit 5 Assessment: Alphabetic Principle pp. 138–139	Unit 5 Assessment: Selection Vocabulary p. 140	Unit 5 Assessment: Comprehension pp. 141–142	Unit 5 Assessment: Grammar, Usage, and Mechanics p. 143

Lesson and Unit Assessment

Unit 6 Class Assessment Record

Student Name	Letter Sounds p. 144	Phoneme Manipulation: Initial and Final Sounds p. 145	Selection Vocabulary p. 146	Classify and Categorize, Story Elements p. 147	Grammar, Usage, and Mechanics p. 148	Letter Sounds p. 149	Phoneme Blending p. 150	Selection Vocabulary p. 151

Lesson and Unit Assessment

Unit 6 Class Assessment Record

Student Name	Compare and Contrast, Text Features p. 152		Grammar, Usage, and Mechanics p. 153	Letter Sounds p. 154	High-Frequency Words p. 155	Selection Vocabulary p. 156	Cause and Effect, Genre Knowledge p. 157		Grammar, Usage, and Mechanics p. 158

Lesson and Unit Assessment

Unit 6 Class Assessment Record

Student Name	Unit 6 Assessment: Phoneme Segmentation p. 160	Unit 6 Assessment: Phoneme Blending p. 161	Unit 6 Assessment: Letter Sounds p. 162	Unit 6 Assessment: Print Concepts p. 163	Unit 6 Assessment: Vocabulary p. 164	Unit 6 Assessment: Comprehension pp. 165–166	Unit 6 Assessment: Grammar, Usage, and Mechanics p. 167

Student Assessment Record

Name_____

Teacher_____ **Grade**_____

Unit/ Lesson	Assessment Name	Date	Number Possible	Number Right	%	Score

SRA
Open Court Reading

Lesson and Unit Assessment

Grade K

Mc Graw Hill

BOOK 1

Open Court Reading

Lesson and Unit Assessment

Grade K

Name _____ **Date** _____ **Score** ___

Phonemic Awareness

1. **yes** **no**

2. **yes** **no**

3. **yes** **no**

4. **yes** **no**

5. **yes** **no**

Name _____ **Date** _____ **Score** _____

Phonemic Awareness

6.

7.

8.

9.

10.

Name _____ **Date** _____ **Score** _____

Phonics and Decoding

1. D   M   R

2. P   T   A

3. M   D   S

4. S   A   K

5. M   P   S

Name _____ **Date** _____ **Score** _____

Phonics and Decoding

6.

7.

8.

9.

10.

Oral Reading Fluency

A   S   D   F   G

H   J   K   L   P

M   N   B   V   O

C   X   Z   Q   W

E   R   T   Y   I

U

Oral Reading Fluency

A   S   D   F   G

H   J   K   L   P

M   N   B   V   O

C   X   Z   Q   W

E   R   Y   T   Y   I

U

Name _____ **Date** _____ **Score** ____

Spelling

Name _____ **Date** _____ **Score** _____

Vocabulary

1. leaf   blue   me

2. fruit   bell   block

3. teacher   brown   angry

4. purple   alphabet   you

5. vegetable   lawn   bus

Name _____ **Date** _____ **Score** _____

Vocabulary

6. proud   block   cousin

7. green   love   I

8. dog   Monday   raspberry

9. April   friend   beside

10. plenty   bucket   dolphin

Comprehension

1. real life   not real life

2. real life   not real life

3. real life   not real life

4. real life   not real life

5. real life   not real life

Comprehension

6. beginning   middle   end

7. beginning   middle   end

8. beginning   middle   end

9. beginning   middle   end

10. beginning   middle   end

Name _____ **Date** _____ **Score** _____

Letter Recognition

d   a   h   c

f   b   g   e

Name _____ **Date** _____ **Score** _____

Selection Vocabulary

1.

2.

3.

4.

5.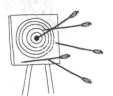

Name _____ **Date** _____ **Score** _____

Main Idea and Details

1.

2.

Story Element: Plot

1.

2.

Name _____ Date _____ Score _____

Grammar, Usage, and Mechanics

1. | woman | yes   no

2. | store | yes   no

3. | farmer | yes   no

4.   Sit   For   Dan

5. Window   Maria   Table

Name _____ **Date** _____ **Score** _____

Letter Recognition

n   i   p   j

m   k   o   l

Name _____ **Date** _____ **Score** _____

Selection Vocabulary

1.

2.

3.

4.

5.

Classify and Categorize

1.

2.

Genre Knowledge and Language Use

1. yes   no

2. nose   coat

Name _____ **Date** _____ **Score** _____

Grammar, Usage, and Mechanics

1. dad   boy   house

2. queen   jar   glove

3. mom   toy   friend

4. doctor   apple   baby

5. sister   button   river

Name _____ **Date** _____ **Score** _____

Letter Recognition

r   u   h   s

t   b   q   e

Name _____ **Date** _____ **Score** _____

Letter Recognition

v   i   p   x

y   k   w   z

Name _____ **Date** _____ **Score** ____

Selection Vocabulary

1.

2.

3.

4.

5.

Assessment

Name _____ Date _____ Score _____

Compare and Contrast

1.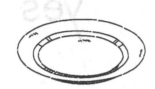

2.

Story Elements

1.

2.

Name _____ **Date** _____ **Score** _____

Grammar, Usage, and Mechanics

1. | school | yes   no

2. | read | yes   no

3. | mother | yes   no

4. | run | yes   no

5. | horse | yes   no

Assessment

Name _____ **Date** _____ **Score** _____

Vocabulary

1. yes   no

2. yes   no

3. yes   no

4. yes   no

5. yes   no

6. yes   no

Name _____ **Date** _____ **Score** _____

Comprehension

1.

2.

3.

4.

5.

Assessment

Name _____ **Date** _____ **Score** _____

Comprehension

6.       

7.       

8.   yes   no

9.   bed   fox

10.   pan   key

Name _____ **Date** _____ **Score** _____

Grammar, Usage, and Mechanics

1. Clock   Alice   Bottle

2. plant   cook   zoo

3. stair   rug   child

4. desert   sailor   button

5. beach   deer   sink

Name _____ **Date** _____ **Score** _____

Counting Words in Sentences

1. 2 3 4

2. 2 3 4

3. 2 3 4

4. 2 3 4

5. 2 3 4

Selection Vocabulary

1.

2.

3.

4.

5.

Name _____ **Date** _____ **Score** _____

Sequence

1.

2.

Genre Knowledge: Folktale

1. yes   no

2. yes   no

Name _____ **Date** _____ **Score** _____

Grammar, Usage, and Mechanics

1. Many stars are in the sky.

2. The dog chased the ball.
   She picked up the ball.
   Then she ran with the ball.

3. run   cloud   blue

4. pretty   beach   swim

5. music   loud   sing

Assessment

Selection Vocabulary

1.

2.

3.

4.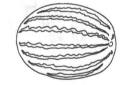

5.

Name _____ **Date** _____ **Score** _____

Cause and Effect

1.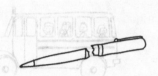

2.

Text Features

1.

2. wonder   friend   tree

Assessment

Name _____ **Date** _____ **Score** _____

Grammar, Usage, and Mechanics

1. the   b   at

2. for   c   g

3. play   dog   and

4. boat   wet   swim

5. tired   pull   down

Selection Vocabulary

1.

2.

3.

4.

5.

Name _____ **Date** _____ **Score** _____

Main Idea and Details

1.

2.

Story Elements

1. yes no

2.

Name _____ Date _____ Score _____

Grammar, Usage, and Mechanics

1. yes   no

2. yes   no

3. yes   no

4. yes   no

5. yes   no

Assessment

Name _____ **Date** _____ **Score** _____

High-Frequency Words

1.	a	had	I
2.	has	he	the
3.	and	a	I
4.	you	he	has
5.	and	has	he

High-Frequency Words

6. one   how   the

7. and   not   all

8. do   go   of

9. see   are   but

10. as   had   by

Name _____ **Date** _____ **Score** _____

Vocabulary

1.   yes   no

2.   yes   no

3.   yes   no

4.   yes   no

5.   yes   no

6.   yes   no

Name _____ **Date** _____ **Score** _____

Comprehension

1.

2.

3.

4.

5.

Assessment

Name _____   **Date** _____   **Score** _____

Comprehension, Genre Knowledge, and Story Elements

6.

7.   yes   no

8.   yes   no

9.

10.   yes   no

Name _____ **Date** _____ **Score** _____

Grammar, Usage, and Mechanics

1. say   no   m

2. Some ducks flew over the pond.

3. skate   cold   ice

4. climb   tree   leaf

5. yes   no

Name _____ Date _____ Score _____

Selection Vocabulary

1.

2.

3.

4.

5.

Classify and Categorize

1.

2.

Text Features

1.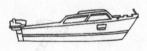

2. yes   no

Assessment

Name _____ Date _____ Score _____

Grammar, Usage, and Mechanics

1. A bird flew by.   2   3   4

2. The car stopped.   2   3   4

3. What time is it?   2   3   4

4. I like cats and dogs.   2   3   4

5. How are you today?   2   3   4

Name _____ **Date** _____ **Date** _____ **Score** _____

Letter Sounds

1. | _it | p   m   s

2. | _ot | s   p   d

3. | ca_ | p   s   m

4. | hi_ | d   m   s

5. | be_ | m   s   d

Assessment

Name _____ **Date** _____ **Score** _____

Selection Vocabulary

1.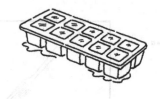

2.

3.

4.

5.

Name _____ Date _____ Score _____

Compare and Contrast

1.

2.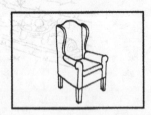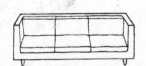

3. yes no

4. yes no

Assessment

Name _____ **Date** _____ **Score** _____

Grammar, Usage, and Mechanics

1. This is a pretty lake

   yes   no

2. When will the game start

   yes   no

3. oceans have salty water.

   yes   no

4. some parks have lakes.

   yes   no

5. That house is very old.

   yes   no

Blending Initial Sounds

1.
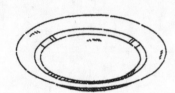  

2.

3.

4.

5.

Name _____ **Date** _____ **Score** _____

High-Frequency Words

1. we   of   am

2. you   am   and

3. go   you   of

4. of   in   he

5. had   has   the

Name _____ **Date** _____ **Score** _____

Selection Vocabulary

1.

2.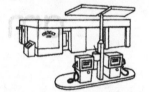

3.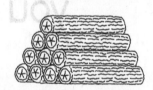

4.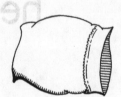

5.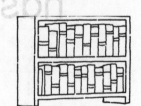

Assessment

Name _____ **Date** _____ **Score** ____

Cause and Effect

1.

2.

Story Elements

1.

2.

Assessment

Name _____ **Date** _____ **Score** _____

Grammar, Usage, and Mechanics

1. a robin is a kind of bird

   yes   no

2. Fish can live under water.

   yes   no

3. A canyon is a kind of deep valley

   yes   no

4. a comet is something in space.

   yes   no

5. Your heart moves blood in your body.

   yes   no

Assessment

Name _____ **Date** _____ **Score** _____

Letters and Sounds

1. d   s   a

2. p   a   m

3. d   a   s

4. p   d   m

5. p   s   a

Name _____ **Date** _____ **Score** ____

Beginning Sounds

1.	sit	sun	pan
2.	dog	mud	milk
3.	pass	at	pet
4.	add	am	sat
5.	dig	pat	dot

Assessment

Name _____ **Date** _____ **Score** _____

Vocabulary

1. yes   no

2. yes   no

3. yes   no

4. yes   no

5. yes   no

6. yes   no

Name _____ **Date** _____ **Score** _____

Comprehension

1.

2.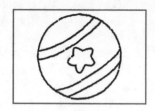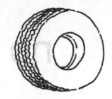

3.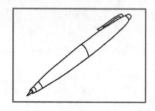

4.

5.

Name _____   Date _____   Score _____

Comprehension, Text Features, and Story Elements

6.

7. **yes**   **no**

8.

9. **yes**   **no**

10. **yes**   **no**

Grammar, Usage, and Mechanics

1.   yes   no

2.   yes   no

3.   Insects have six legs.

     yes   no

4.   water freezes when it gets cold.

     yes   no

5.   A baby frog is a tadpole

     yes   no

Name _____ **Date** _____ **Score** _____

Selection Vocabulary

1.

2.

3.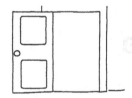

4.

5.

Name _____ **Date** _____ **Score** _____

Main Idea and Details

1.

2.

Genre Knowledge

1. yes   no

2. yes   no

Assessment

Name _____ **Date** _____ **Score** _____

Grammar, Usage, and Mechanics

1. yes   no

2. yes   no

3. yes   no

4. yes   no

5. yes   no

Name _____ **Date** _____ **Score** _____

Letter Sounds

1. | _at | m   h   p

2. | _et | s   n   l

3. | _ap | n   c   m

4. | bu_ | s   t   n

5. | he_ | n   d   s

Assessment

Name _____ **Date** _____ **Score** _____

Selection Vocabulary

1.

2.

3.

4.

5.   yes   no

Name _____ **Date** _____ **Score** _____

Sequence

1.

2.

Text Features

1.   yes   no

2.   yes   no

Name _____ Date _____ Score _____

Grammar, Usage, and Mechanics

1. | A bird has feathers. | yes no

2. | ceiling | yes no

3. | basement | yes no

4. . ? !

5. . ? !

Name _____ Date _____ Score _____

Short-Vowel Sounds

1. p_t   a   i

2. h_d   a   i

3. _t   a   i

4. r_n   a   i

5. l_p   a   i

Assessment

Name _____ **Date** _____ **Score** _____

High-Frequency Words

1. had   has   have

2. as   to   it

3. it   am   is

4. go   to   you

5. in   a   at

Name _____ **Date** _____ **Score** _____

High-Frequency Words

had   in   the   is   and

Scoring:

☐ had   ☐ in   ☐ the   ☐ is   ☐ and   Total: ___

☐ Student read words at a pace that suggests they were recognized automatically.

Assessment

Name _____ **Date** _____ **Score** _____

Selection Vocabulary

1.

2.

3.

4.

5. yes   no

Name _____ Date _____ Score _____

Cause and Effect

1.

2.

Story Elements

1.

2.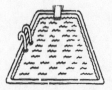

Name _____ Date _____ Score _____

Grammar, Usage, and Mechanics

1. yes   no

2. yes   no

3. yes   no

4. yes   no

5. yes   no

Name _____ **Date** _____ **Score** _____

Letters and Sounds

1. m   h   i

2. t   g   h

3. s   m   n

4. h   n   l

5. i   l   a

Name _____ Date _____ Score _____

Vocabulary

1.   yes   no

2.   yes   no

3.   yes   no

4.   yes   no

5.   yes   no

6.   yes   no

Name _____ Date _____ Score _____

Comprehension

1.

2.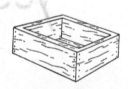

3.

4.

5.

Assessment

Name _____ **Date** _____ **Score** _____

Comprehension

6. yes   no

7. yes   no

8. yes   no

9. | 2   3

10.

Name _____ **Date** _____ **Score** _____

Grammar, Usage, and Mechanics

1. garage   The light is on.

2. This is my hat.   shovel

3.   How far away is the moon

      yes   no

4.   yes   no

5.   yes   no

Name _____ **Date** _____ **Score** _____

Selection Vocabulary

1.

2.

3.

4.

5.

Name _____ **Date** _____ **Score** _____

Classify and Categorize

1.

2.

Text Features and Language Use

1.  yes no

2. ? !

Assessment

Name _____ Date _____ Score _____

Grammar, Usage, and Mechanics

1. **yes**   **no**

2. **yes**   **no**

3. What is the name of that star

   yes   **no**

4. Wow, that is a great story you wrote

   yes   **no**

5. That cloud is a nimbus cloud

   yes   **no**

Selection Vocabulary

1.

      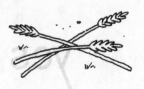

2.

3.

4.

5.

Assessment

Name _____ **Date** _____ **Score** _____

Main Idea and Details

1.

2.

Language Use

1.   .   ?   !

2.   yes   no

Name _____ **Date** _____ **Score** _____

Grammar, Usage, and Mechanics

1.   yes   no

2.   yes   no

3.   That is wonderful news

        yes   no

4.   yes   no

5.   yes   no

        Assessment

Name _____   **Date** _____   **Score** _____

Letter Sounds

1. | __ot | h   g   s

2. | __an | c   m   t

3. | __ed | l   b   r

4. | le__ | d   g   t

5. | ru__ | b   n   g

Name _____ **Date** _____ **Score** ____

High-Frequency Words

can   his   on   him   did

Scoring:

☐ can ☐ his ☐ on ☐ him ☐ did Total: ___

☐ Student read words at a pace that suggests they were recognized automatically.

Assessment

Name _____ **Date** _____ **Score** _____

Selection Vocabulary

1.

2.

3.

4.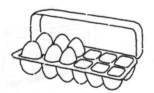

5.

Name _____ **Date** _____ **Score** _____

Sequence

1.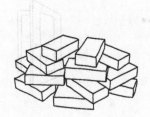

2.

Text Features and Story Elements

1.

2.

Assessment

Name _____ **Date** _____ **Score** _____

Grammar, Usage, and Mechanics

1. Be careful, the dish is hot!

yes   no

2. Pears grow on trees!

yes   no

3. Surprise, here's your present.

yes   no

4. Get out of the way of that car!

yes   no

5. Mars is a planet near Earth.

yes   no

Assessment

Name _____ **Date** _____ **Score** _____

Letter Sounds

1.   c   r   g

2.   b   d   t

3.   a   i   o

4.   r   b   s

5.   h   g   s

Name _____   **Date** _____   **Score** _____

Alphabetic Principle

1.   g   c   b

2.   p   b   d

3.   g   d   t

4.   t   c   g

5.   p   m   n

Name _____ **Date** _____ **Score** _____

Alphabetic Principle

6.   b   m   p

7.   d   g   t

8.   g   c   s

9.   r   c   s

10.   r   i   g

Assessment

Name _____ Date _____ Score _____

Vocabulary

1. yes   no

2. yes   no

3. yes   no

4. yes   no

5. yes   no

6. yes   no

Name _____ **Date** _____ **Score** _____

Comprehension

1.

2.

3.

4.

5.

Name _____ **Date** _____ **Score** _____

Comprehension

6.    yes   no

7.   

8.    

9.   .   ?   !

10.   .   ?   !

Name _____ **Date** _____ **Score** _____

Grammar, Usage, and Mechanics

1.   yes   no

2.   yes   no

3.   Here is your lunch!

      yes   no

4.   yes   no

5.   .   !   ?

Name _____ **Date** _____ **Score** _____

Selection Vocabulary

1.       

2.    

3.      

4.       

5.    

Name _____ Date _____ Score _____

Classify and Categorize

1.

2.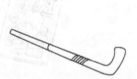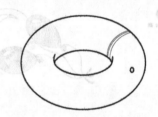

Story Elements

1.

2.

Name _____ Date _____ Score _____

Grammar, Usage, and Mechanics

1. The sun was setting.I watched the sunset.

   yes   no

2. Is it cold outside? You might need a coat.

   yes   no

3. The moon shined. We gazed at it.

   yes   no

4. Bowling is fun!We go every week.

   yes   no

5. The bus is late.Will it be here soon?

   yes   no

Selection Vocabulary

1.

2.

3.

4.

5.

Assessment

Name _____ **Date** _____ **Score** _____

Compare and Contrast

1.

2.

Text Features

1.   .   !

2. "This is wonderful soup," said Raj.
   His father smiled at him.

Assessment

Grammar, Usage, and Mechanics

1. # yes ## no

2. # yes ## no

3.

4.

5.

Assessment

Name _____ **Date** _____ **Score** _____

Letter Sounds

1. 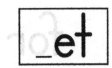   j   g   r

2.    h   m   f

3. 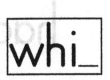   m   u   c

4. fi_   x   n   c

5. whi_   m   z   t

Name _____ **Date** _____ **Score** _____

High-Frequency Words

1. of   all   for

2. but   am   go

3. do   up   of

4. all   at   am

5. his   girl   had

Assessment

Name _____   Date _____   Score _____

Selection Vocabulary

1.

2.

3.

4.

5.

Name _____ **Date** _____ **Score** _____

Cause and Effect

1.

2.

Genre Knowledge

1. yes   no

2. yes   no

Assessment

Name _____ **Date** _____ **Score** _____

Grammar, Usage, and Mechanics

1. The game started at noon.

   2   3   4

2. Bob saw Dot. He waved to her. She came over. They talked for a bit.

   2   3   4

3. Our flag has stars and stripes.

   yes   no

4. yes   no

5. yes   no

Name _____ **Date** _____ **Score** _____

Vocabulary

1.   yes   no

2.   yes   no

3.   yes   no

4.   yes   no

5.   yes   no

6.   yes   no

Name _____ **Date** _____ **Score** _____

Comprehension

1.

2.

3.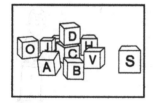

4.

5.

Name _____ **Date** _____ **Score** _____

Comprehension

6. ## yes ## no

7.

8.

9. **.** **?**  **!**

10. **.** **?** **!**

Assessment

Name _____ **Date** _____ **Score** ____

Grammar, Usage, and Mechanics

1. Small fish swam in the pond.

    3   4   5

2. Bart threw the ball to Laura. She caught it and threw it back to him.

    | 2   3

3. can I borrow your pen?

    yes   no

4.   yes   no

5.   yes   no

Assessment

Grammar, Usage, and Mechanics

1. Small fish swam in the pond.

3   4   5

2. Bart threw the the ball to Laura. She caught it
and threw it back to him.

1   2   3

3. can I borrow your pen?

yes   no

4. yes   no

5. yes   no